Mitra Mann is a specialist litigator in Contentious Probate and Court of Protection disputes. She deals with cases involving Will disputes, claims for reasonable financial provisions from an estate, professional negligence, restoring a vulnerable person's estate and a range of Court of Protection applications.

Mitra is particularly passionate about protecting vulnerable adults. She is a trained Dementia Friends Champion dedicated to raising awareness of mental capacity issues locally and nationally. One way of preventing financial abuse, whether done intentionally or unintentionally, is to share information with other professionals, carers, financial advisers, attorneys and deputies and to that end, Mitra has written articles and delivered webinars and seminars in several Court of Protection practice areas.

Court of Protection:

A Practical Guide to Gifting

Court of Protection:

A Practical Guide to Gifting

Mitra Mann

LLB (Hons)

PGDip in Legal Practice

PGCert in Medical Law and Ethics

Law Brief Publishing

Published 2024 by Law Brief Publishing, an imprint of Law Brief Publishing Ltd
30 The Parks
Minehead
Somerset
TA24 8BT

www.lawbriefpublishing.com

Paperback: 978-1-914608-64-3

To my parents

Dan and Manju Bundhoo

You remain my source of strength,
determination and inspiration.

PREFACE

One of the clearest ways in which the power given to an attorney[1] or a deputy[2] can be misused is by giving away the assets of a protected person - who the author will refer to as "P" in this book. There appears to be a general lack of awareness, particularly amongst lay attorneys and deputies, of the scope of their powers and authority. From her own experience over the past years as well as from the cases heard in the Court of Protection, the author has identified 2 main misconceptions which tend to influence an attorney's or a deputy's decision:

1) They believe they can do whatever they like with P's assets once they are appointed;

2) They feel that they should do whatever P could or would have done if they had capacity.

The purpose of this book is primarily to help lay attorneys and deputies understand the extent of their powers and when to refer matters to the Court of Protection. It is also the author's aim to assist practitioners who regularly advise attorneys and deputies on the management of P's property and affairs.

Although there is a logical sequence to the chapters in this book, it has been written so that it can be read in any order, depending on who the reader is: whether it is an attorney or a deputy familiarising themselves

---

[1] For the purposes of this book, an "attorney" or "attorneys" is someone appointed by a donor to make make decisions regarding their property and affairs only (and not to make health and welfare decisions).

[2] For the purposes of this book, a "deputy" or "deputies" is someone appointed by the Court of Protection to make decisions regarding P's property and affairs only (and not to make health and welfare decisions).

with their powers or a practitioner navigating their way through the complexities of Court of Protection proceedings.

This book is by no means the main authority on the gifting of P's assets. It is recommended that practitioners, attorneys and deputies refer to other sources of information and materials including the Mental Capacity Act 2005, the Mental Capacity Act 2005 Code of Practice, the Court of Protection Rules 2017 as well as the Public Guardian's Guidance[3] and Practice Note[4] on giving gifts.

The law quoted in this book was believed to be correct at 30 November 2023.

I have used examples from my professional experience combined with other scenarios to create fictitious case studies in this book.

Mitra Mann
January 2024

---

[3] OPG2.

[4] Practice Note PN7.

GLOSSARY

Protected person (P) – a person who lacks the mental capacity to make certain decisions because of an impairment of, or disturbance in the functioning of their mind or brain.

Attorney – someone who is chosen and appointed by another person (known as a Donor) to make certain decisions on their behalf.

Code of Practice – guidance which supports the Mental Capacity Act 2005 and explains how this legislation should be interpreted and implemented when making decisions on behalf of P.

Court of Protection (COP) – a specialist Court established in 2007 which makes specific decisions on behalf of or relating to P; or appoints other people known as deputies to make decisions on behalf of P.

Mental Capacity Act 2005 (MCA 2005) – legislation which came into effect on 1 October 2007 making provisions relating to and to protect those who lack the capacity to make decisions (P).

Office of the Public Guardian (OPG) – a government body, working within the framework of the Mental Capacity Act 2005, that maintains a register of attorneys, deputies and guardians. Part of the Public Guardian's role involves supporting and supervising attorneys and deputies; investigating concerns regarding their actions; and taking steps deemed necessary to protect P's interests.

Official Solicitor (OS) – part of the Ministry of Justice acting for those who are unable to represent themselves in court proceedings. The OS would normally be appointed if P does not have a litigation friend or there is not anyone suitable to represent P's interests in a court case.

CONTENTS

INTRODUCTION

THE COURT OF PROTECTION AND THE MENTAL CAPACITY ACT 2005

This chapter sets out the background to the evolving laws relating to a protected person ("P"). Its purpose is to help readers have a broad understanding of the developments in this specialist field which eventually led to the passing of the Mental Capacity Act 2005.

The notion of "P" is not a recent one. Throughout times, it has been recognised that some individuals lack the capacity to make certain decisions and therefore require assistance. The Lunacy Act 1890 gave various powers to the Court of Protection (subsequently named as such in 1947) over an individual who was incapable, by reason of a mental disorder, of managing and administering their property and affairs. In such instances, a person known as a "Receiver" was appointed to handle P's affairs under the supervision of the Court of Protection.

Unsurprisingly, the Court of Protection struggled to keep up with the financial affairs of all mentally incapacitated persons in the country. After several consultations, a simpler procedure was put in place by passing the Enduring Powers of Attorney Act in 1985 which enabled a "Donor", whilst they still had capacity, to create and give powers to an attorney of their choice. The Donor could choose someone to help them manage their financial affairs- even after they lost capacity (making it different to an Ordinary Power of Attorney which comes to an end upon the Donor losing capacity) – and there was no requirement for the attorney to be under the supervision of the Court of Protection. This provided some relief to the Court of Protection.

However, it was not long before several deficiencies were identified. One of the key aspects of an Enduring Power of Attorney is that there was no requirement for it to be registered with the Office of the Public Guardian before it could be used. [1] The attorney was only required to register the Enduring Power of Attorney when "*the donor is or is becoming mentally incapable.*"[2] But who decided when the Donor had lost or was losing capacity? This became a grey area.

The approach of legal and medical professionals was to concentrate on the Donor's medical condition rather than its effects on them. An "*all or nothing*" approach was known to be adopted. Many attorneys did not register the Enduring Power of Attorney and remained "off" the radar of the Office of the Public Guardian. Since the Court of Protection had stopped overseeing the management of P's finances following the enactment of the Enduring Powers of Attorney Act 1985, this created a vacuum – the Office of the Public Guardian did not have the attorneys on their register, nor was the Court of Protection overseeing them. It was not long before a rise in financial abuse taking place was noted.

This prompted the consideration of the whole question of decision-making and mental incapacity. It became clear that reform was needed together with a comprehensive structure on how to assess capacity. The Mental Capacity Act 2005 subsequently came into effect in October 2007, setting out clearly the parameters of capacity and decision-making.

1 This is one of the main differences between an Enduring Power of Attorney and a Lasting Power of Attorney. There is a requirement for a Lasting Power of Attorney to be registered with the Office of the Public Guardian before it can be used.

2 See Part C of an Enduring Power of Attorney instrument.

CHAPTER ONE

CAPACITY: WHEN DOES ONE BECOME "P"?

Capacity is key when making an application to the Court of Protection. This is because the Court of Protection will only consider cases where the person involved has, on the balance of probabilities, lost the capacity to make the decision in question.

Mr Justice Hayden's judgment in the case of **PH v Betsi Cadwaladr University Health Board** [2022] [3] is a helpful reminder of this. In his words, "*The Court has no business in telling capacitious individuals what is in their best interests nor any locus from which to compel others to bend to the will either of what capacitious individuals may want or what the court might consider they require. Such a regime would be fundamentally unhealthy in a mature democratic society and would have the collateral impact of undermining the principle of autonomy which is central to the philosophy of the MCA.*"[4]

> Author's note – There are instances when someone may not necessarily lack capacity but is considered to be vulnerable. The Court of Protection will not hear such cases but the High Court's inherent jurisdiction can be invoked. However, the High Court will only intervene where there is a demonstrated need to protect a vulnerable person from abuse or the real possibility of abuse. The risk of future possible abuse must be a "*real*" possibility and not a "*fanciful*" risk.

3 PH v Betsi Cadwaladr University Health Board [2022] EWCOP 16 (31 March 2022).

4 PH v Betsi Cadwaladr University Health Board [2022] EWCOP 16, para 19.

This takes readers to the next section – if the Court of Protection will only intervene in cases where P lacks capacity, how is P's capacity (or lack of) determined before an application is made to the Court of Protection?

1.1 – P's capacity pre-Mental Capacity Act 2005

Prior to the Mental Capacity Act 2005, English common law adopted a basic test to determine capacity. This involved considering whether the person concerned understood, in broad terms, what they were doing and the implications of their actions.

Over time, different capacity tests were developed in respect of specific decisions[5] – such as the making of a Will (**Banks v Goodfellow**[6] in 1870); gifting (**Re Beany**[7] in 1978); deciding on a place of residence and having contact with others (**Re MB (Medical Treatment)**[8] in 1997); engaging in litigation (**Masterman-Lister v Brutton and Co**[9] in 2002); or entering into a marriage contract (**Sheffield City Council v E & Anor**[10] in 2004).

5 Listed in the Mental Capacity Act 2005 Code of Practice, chapter 4.

6 Banks v Goodfellow (1870) LR 5 QB 549.

7 Re Beaney [1978] 1 WLR 770.

8 Re MB (Treatment) [1997] EWCA Civ 3093 (26 March 1997).

9 Masterman-Lister v Brutton and Co [2002] EWCA Civ 1889 (19 December 2002).

10 Sheffield City Council v E & Anor [2004] EWHC 2808 (Fam) (02 December 2004).

Author's note to practitioners in the Chancery Division of the High Court – the Mental Capacity Act 2005 has not replaced the common law tests. The Mental Capacity 2005 Code of Practice states that "*The Act's new definition of capacity is in line with the existing common law tests, and the Act does not replace them. When cases come before the court on the above issues, judges can adopt the new definition if they think it is appropriate.*"[11] The Mental Capacity Act 2005 is there to "supplement" the common law tests and to be used as a "cross-check". Common law tests therefore still apply when bringing a case in the Chancery Division.

1.2 – P's capacity post Mental Capacity Act 2005 and the presumption of capacity

The Mental Capacity Act 2005 introduced 5 main principles:

1. *A person must be assumed to have capacity unless it is established that he lacks capacity.*

2. *A person is not to be treated as unable to make a decision unless all practicable steps to help him to do so have been taken without success.*

3. *A person is not to be treated as unable to make a decision merely because he makes an unwise decision.*

4. *An act done, or decision made, under this Act for or on behalf of a person who lacks capacity must be done, or made, in his best interests.*

5. *Before the act is done, or the decision is made, regard must be had to whether the purpose for which it is needed can be as effectively*

11 Mental Capacity Act 2005, section 1.

> *achieved in a way that is less restrictive of the person's rights and freedom of action.*[12]

It is recommended that readers familiarise themselves with these principles. The author will focus on the first principle in this section since it is of particular importance that lay attorneys and deputies understand the risks of drawing generalised conclusions on P's capacity.

One of the key features of the Mental Capacity Act 2005 is that there is a *presumption of capacity*. The starting point, therefore, is that one has the capacity to make a decision for themselves unless there is evidence to suggest otherwise. This presumption is clearly stated in section 1(2) of the Mental Capacity Act 2005: *"A person must be assumed to have capacity unless it is established that he lacks capacity."*

Accordingly, all adults must be presumed to be competent until the contrary is proven and the burden of proof rests on those asserting incapacity. Evidence of P's incapacity is therefore key to any application made to the Court of Protection. Should there not be convincing evidence regarding P's incapacity, the Court of Protection will refrain from making a best-interests decision on behalf of P.[13]

The Mental Capacity Act 2005 also sets out clear parameters when it comes to defining those who lack capacity. A person is deemed as lacking capacity in relation to a matter if "*at all material times he is unable to make a decision for himself in relation to the matter because of an impairment of, or a disturbance in the functioning of, the mind or brain.*"[14]

Some practitioners reading this section may relate to the follow scenario: you are approached by a prospective client who has already formed the

12 See Mental Capacity Act 2005, section 1(2)-(6).

13 See Chapter 1 – the case of PH v Betsi Cadwaladr University Health Board [2022].

14 Mental Capacity Act 2005, section 2(1).

view that someone they know has been diagnosed with dementia and therefore lacks capacity. As a matter of course, you should put the following question to the prospective client: "*What decision do they lack the capacity to make?*" This is because there is not a blanket approach to capacity under the Mental Capacity Act 2005. Different levels of capacity are required for different activities or transactions. This is not a novel concept as evidenced by the various common law tests developed over the years.[15]

1.3 – Different levels of capacity for different decisions: case law

The importance of understanding and differentiating between the different decisions in question was highlighted in the case of **A, B and C v X, Y and Z [2012]**[16] which came before Mr Justice Hedley in the Court of Protection. It is recommended that readers review the detailed judgment which is a very helpful tool to use when analysing the various legal tests on capacity, including P's fluctuating capacity.

In this case, the Court of Protection was required to determine whether P had the capacity to make a series of decisions, in particular, the decision to:

(i) marry;

(ii) make a Will;

(iii) revoke or grant a power of attorney;

(iv) manage his affairs;

(v) litigate; and

15 See Chapter 1.1 for the various common law tests.

16 A, B and C v X, Y and Z [2012] EWHC 2400 (COP).

(vi) decide with whom he has contact.

This case involved P, a skilled and highly intelligent man, whose former wife had died in April 2008. P and his wife had been married for 56 years and her death was a great shock to him. Following his wife's death, in May 2008, P was diagnosed with dementia. A few months later, in September 2008, P made Lasting Powers of Attorney appointing his three children as his attorneys.

A carer came on the scene in 2010 and in October 2010, P expressed the wish to marry the carer. This caused conflicts between P and his children resulting in court proceedings to determine P's capacity to make decisions.

Evidence from two psychiatrists, Professor Jacoby and Dr Prabhakaran, were obtained. The psychiatrists differed in their assessment of P's capacity. Further evidence from Dr Poz, a neuropsychologist, was obtained and he remained neutral. Ultimately, P's capacity to make the decisions in question was a matter for the Court of Protection to determine.

After considering the main principles set out in the Mental Capacity Act 2005, the medical and witness evidence as well as the facts before him, Mr Justice Hedley found that (using the same numbering as above in respect of the specific decisions):

(i) the applicants failed to satisfy the Court that P lacked the capacity to marry;

(ii) P had a "qualified"[17] capacity when it came to testamentary capacity. Mr Justice Hedley could not make a general declaration regarding testamentary capacity and commented

17 The Judge alluded to borderline capacity and found that there will undoubtedly be times when P lacks capacity just as there will also be many times when he retains it.

that as a result, any Will made by P, if unaccompanied by contemporaneous medical evidence asserting capacity, would be seriously open to challenge;

(iii) P had "qualified"[18] capacity when it came to making and/or revoking a power of attorney and once again, unless accompanied by contemporaneous medical evidence of capacity, this would give rise to a serious risk of challenge or refusal to register;

(iv) in light of Dr Poz's evidence, on the balance of probabilities, P lacked the capacity to manage his own affairs;

(v) although there are aspects of the case that P could understand and follow, P lacked the capacity to conduct the litigation in question. [19]

Determining capacity is not as simple as it may initially seem and general assumptions should not be made. The above case is an example of the various issues at play and a stark reminder that the Court of Protection will not adopt a blanket approach when it comes to P's capacity. Each and every decision will be reviewed separately before a declaration is made in respect of the decision in question.

---

18 See footnote 21.

19 A, B and C v X, Y and Z [2012] EWHC 2400 (COP) (Reported Judgment), paras 37-45.

1.4 – Case study

Richard is a widower and was diagnosed with dementia 2 years ago. His condition is gradually deteriorating. Recently, Richard's son, David, has noticed that when discussing his affairs, Richard often gets confused regarding the ownership of his house and who he would like to leave his assets to after his death since he has not made a Will. Even though Richard often gets confused, his life has not changed much and he is managing just as he was before. However, David is concerned. Since his father never made a Power of Attorney, you are asked by David to advise on whether a deputy should be appointed to manage Richard's finances and a statutory will should be considered.

In the above scenario, the following assumptions are likely to be made by David:

(i) Richard has been diagnosed with dementia and therefore no longer has the capacity to make decisions.

(ii) Richard should not be handling his finances and a deputy should be appointed in the absence of a Power of Attorney.

(iii) An application is now required for a statutory will.

These are common pitfalls which should be avoided and the author sets out below how a matter such as this one should be addressed.

Assumption 1: Richard has been diagnosed with dementia and therefore no longer has the capacity to make decisions.

Whilst it is recognised that developing a form of dementia or sustaining a brain injury can impair the functioning of the brain, the diagnosis of a medical condition itself does not automatically render someone incapable of making decisions for themselves. Readers are reminded that under the Mental Capacity Act 2005, there is a presumption that Richard has capacity.

It is noted that Richard is managing just as he was before. It would be wrong for David to assume that his father is no longer capable to make decisions regarding his property and affairs without any evidence to the contrary. However, it is also recognised that given the nature of Richard's progressive illness, his capacity to manage his finances is likely to diminish over time. David should be advised, at this early stage, to support his father in making decisions (if such support is needed) and keep matters under regular review.

Assumption 2: Richard should not be handling his finances and a deputy should be appointed in the absence of a Power of Attorney.

Appointing a deputy simply because Richard has been diagnosed with dementia would be premature. The focus should be on what decision is being contemplated at this present time and whether Richard is able to make it. *This is because capacity is decision and time specific.*

If Richard retains the capacity to make decisions regarding his affairs despite his diagnosis, it would be sensible, at this stage, for David to discuss and explore with his father the possibility of making a Lasting Power of Attorney and plan for the future. If Richard has the capacity to make a Lasting Power of Attorney and proceeds with making one, it is advisable for the practitioner and/or the certificate provider[20] to keep a clear record of how Richard's capacity was assessed and the conclusion reached.

However, Richard may decide not to make a Lasting Power of Attorney at this present time. As time goes by, Richard may find that he is no longer able to manage all his affairs but finds himself capable of purchasing his grocery and paying for day-to-day modest expenses. At this point, David should seek a report on Richard's capacity to manage his property and affairs. If the report concludes that Richard no longer has the capacity to manage his finances, then making an application to

20 See section 10 of a Lasting Power of Attorney instrument and the statement given by a certificate provider.

the Court of Protection for the appointment of a deputy would be in Richard's best interests. This is when it would be justifiable for David to take the necessary steps to ensure that a deputy is appointed to manage his father's finances.

Author's note – Capacity is not merely decision-specific. It is also specific in relation to different transactions of the same type of decision. In this case study, it would appear that Richard retains some level of capacity to manage his finances since he is able to pay for small expenses. Even after a deputy is appointed, the deputy should assist Richard with making smaller decisions regarding his finances, such as providing him with a weekly allowance to manage his outgoings. *It is important not to strip Richard/P of all their freedom.*

Assumption 3: An application is now required for a statutory will.

It is important to remind David that there are 2 separate decisions being contemplated: whether Richard can (i) manage his financial affairs and (ii) make a Will. As mentioned in Chapter 1.4, a blanket approach to Richard's capacity should not be applied.

A separate report should be sought regarding Richard's testamentary capacity. A report which concludes that Richard lacks the capacity to manage his financial affairs does not necessarily mean that Richard cannot make a Will. The author has seen medical reports confirming that P has the capacity to make a Will but lacks the capacity to manage their finances. This may come as a surprise to some readers but it is not unexpected given that different levels of understanding are required for different decisions.[21] For instance, the level of understanding required to make a simple and straightforward Will is likely to be lower than the level of understanding required to manage an investment portfolio involving

21 See Chapter 1.3 – the case of A, B and C v X, Y and Z [2012] EWHC 2400 (COP) (Reported Judgment).

numerous stocks and shares.

If the report concludes that Richard lacks testamentary capacity, an application for a statutory will can be made if it is considered to be in Richard's best interests to do so.[22]

22 Readers are advised to go through the decision-making process which is addressed in Chapter 6 and seek advice before making a statutory will application.

CHAPTER TWO

P'S CAPACITY TO MAKE A GIFT

As mentioned in the previous chapter, there is a presumption of capacity and the burden of proof rests with those asserting incapacity. In this chapter, the author will address P's capacity to make gifts before going into detail on the gifts which attorneys and deputies can make on behalf of P once it is determined that P lacks the capacity to make such gifts.

2.1 – The common law test

The common law test to determine an individual's capacity to make a gift is set out in the case of **Re Beany** [1978][23]. In this case, the Judge referred to the principle stated in general terms by the House of Lords in **Ball v Mannin** (1829)[24] that "*the person concerned is capable of understanding what he does by executing the deed in question when its general purport has fully been explained to him.*"[25]

In the case of **Re Beaney,** the Judge considered the arguments advanced by the parties and whether a "narrow view" or a "wider view" should be considered when determining what degree of understanding Mrs Beaney required before transferring her house to her daughter. The Judge thought it necessary for Mrs Beaney to understand that she was in fact disposing of the whole of her estate and to appreciate the claims of the other potential beneficiaries, namely, her two other children might have

---

23 Re Beaney [1978] 1 WLR 770

24 Ball v. Mannin (1829) 3 Bli.N.S. 1. This case dealt with the test with regard to deeds.

25 Re Beaney [1978] 1 WLR 770, para 773.

against her estate.[26] The Judge in this case also made the point that the amount of the gift in question has a bearing on how capacity should be assessed. If the gift in question is substantial or comprises the majority of P's estate (for example the gift is P's house which is the main asset of their estate), then a higher degree of understanding will be required. In such a case, the **Banks v Goodfellow [1870]**[27] test will apply despite being a test to determine testamentary capacity. In brief, the Banks v Goodfellow test involves P:

i. understanding the nature of their act and its effects;

ii. understanding the extent and value of the property/assets in their estate which they are disposing of;

iii. appreciating that others may make a claim against their estate if they are not provided for; and

iv. is not suffering from a disorder of the mind which is poisoning or affecting their senses.

2.2 – Which legal test to use: the common law test or the Mental Capacity Act 2005 test?

Whilst the common law test set out in **Re Beaney [1978]**[28] still applies to cases in the High Court when the making of a lifetime gift is being challenged, practitioners are reminded that for the purposes of making an application to the Court of Protection, the legal test set out in section 3 (1) (a)-(d) of the Mental Capacity Act 2005 will apply.

Section 3(1) of the Mental Capacity Act 2005 states that a person is

26 Re Beaney [1978] 1 WLR 770, para 773.

27 Banks v Goodfellow (1870) LR 5 QB 549.

28 Re Beaney [1978] 1 WLR 770.

unable to make a decision for himself if he is unable:

(a) to understand the information relevant to the decision,

(b) to retain that information,

(c) to use or weigh that information as part of the process of making the decision, or

(d) to communicate his decision (whether by talking, using sign language or any other means).

These are the main points which an expert will be expected to address when reporting on P's capacity to make a gift prior to an application being made to the Court of Protection. This has been the case since the introduction of the Mental Capacity Act 2005. Practitioners should therefore set out clearly to the expert which legal test they should apply when preparing a contemporaneous report on P's capacity to make a gift. Even though there is a notable overlap between section 3 of the Mental Capacity Act 2005 and the two common law tests set out in **Re Beaney** [**1978**] and **Banks v Goodfellow** [**1870**], the expert's focus should be on the requirements set out in section 3 of the Mental Capacity Act 2005. However, depending on the facts of the case, the instructing practitioner should consider whether an assessment based on the Mental Capacity Act 2005 combined with the common law test is appropriate.

2.3 – Who can assess capacity?

There is no requirement for a specific medical expert or professional to carry out an assessment. The assessor must, however, have the proper training and credentials and must also be an impartial and qualified person. The Mental Capacity Act 2005 Code of Practice lists several professionals who can carry out such an assessment.[29] Such professionals

29 Mental Capacity Code of Conduct 2007, para 4.42.

include P's GP or the consultant under whose care P is; an approved mental health professional; a social worker; a psychiatrist, a psychologist, a speech and language therapist or an occupational therapist. It is advisable to check the expert's credentials, qualifications and experience before deciding on whether they are the appropriate expert to assess P.

In cases where a substantial gift is being considered and P is under the care of a specialist or a consultant, it is advisable to instruct the consultant to prepare the report since they are likely to have had regular contact with P and will therefore be in a better position to give an opinion. Alternatively, there are several known mental capacity assessors based all over England and Wales who are willing to travel to P and prepare the relevant report. These assessors are normally qualified in preparing reports of this nature and a copy of their CV and qualifications should be considered carefully before they are instructed.

2.4 – The Letter of Instructions

The author finds the Assessment Tool prepared by STEP (Mental Capacity Special Interest Group)[30] helpful and recommends that readers refer to it before instructing an expert.

To assist the mental capacity assessor with preparing their report, it is advisable to prepare a detailed letter of instructions. The letter of instructions should set out the two-stage test to assess P's capacity. This involves the assessor looking at whether:

1) There is an impairment of or disturbance in the functioning of the person's mind or brain. If there is, then the assessor should proceed to the second stage, also known as the *functional test:*

2) Is the impairment or disturbance sufficient that P lacks the

30 Mental Capacity Assessment Tool for Decision of: Capacity to Make a Lifetime Gift.

capacity to make the particular decision?[31]

The letter of instructions should also address the following:

- A reminder that the assessor must apply the five statutory principles of the Mental Capacity Act 2005[32] and an explanation as to what they are.
- A reminder that the standard of proof required should be based on the balance of probabilities.
- An explanation as to why the application is being made to the Court of Protection.
- Provide background information on P's family dynamics and who the proposed gift is being made to.
- Inform the assessor of any other factor which may affect P's reasoning such as a recent bereavement or if P has been suffering from depression.
- Provide details of P's illness, diagnosis, prognosis and life expectancy.
- Provide details of P's assets, income and expenditure given that the decision in question involves P's finances.
- If known, set out P's history of gifting and his intentions – this includes providing any written documents previously prepared

---

31 The expert should have regard to section 3(1) (a)-(d) of the Mental Capacity Act 2005 when carrying out their assessment.

32 Mental capacity Act 2005, section 1.

by P or witness statements from P's family and friends whom P had previously discussed this issue with.

- Provide a copy of P's medical notes, if relevant.

- Suggest that the assessor talks to P about wider issues (based on the information provided as set out above) and ask open questions to assess the degree of P's understanding. Their questions should not be limited to "Yes" or "No" answers.

- Provide information on known communication tools and practical steps which should be used to assist P with participating in the assessment, such as using sign language or visiting P at a specific time when they are more likely to be alert.

- Seek an estimate of the assessor's fee and the timescale within which an assessment will take place and the report written up.

In most cases, form COP3[33] will be attached to the Letter of Instructions which the assessor will be required to complete. This form sets out the key information which the Court of Protection will have regard to when making a best-interests decision.

---

33 A copy of form COP3 can be downloaded at: https://www.gov.uk/government/publications/make-a-report-on-someones-capacity-to-make-decisions-form-cop3. This form was updated in July 2023. See Chapter 8.6 for further details on completing form COP3.

CHAPTER THREE

GIFTING ON BEHALF OF P AND MAINTENANCE PAYMENTS

For the purposes of this chapter, it will be assumed that P no longer has the capacity to make gifts and their attorney or deputy is considering making a gift on their behalf.

It can be easily assumed by attorneys and deputies that a gift is simply the transfer of P's money to someone else. As such, they might form the view that legal advice or the Court of Protection's approval is not required if the transaction being contemplated does not involve the transfer of P's money. It is crucial for attorneys and deputies to have a firm understanding of what constitutes a gift.

3.1 – What is a gift?

As mentioned above, a gift is not simply a monetary transaction. It has a wider definition and according to the Oxford Popular English Dictionary, a gift is "*a thing given, a present.*" A gift can therefore take several shapes and forms – it is not limited to money or a specific asset.

The Office of the Public Guardian has published a guide for attorneys and deputies which sets out examples of what counts as a gift.[34] The author repeats a few of these examples below to give readers a flavour of the wider definition of a "gift":

34 OPG2: Giving gifts for someone else.

- Payment of someone's school fees or university fees (even though there is a history of P doing so).
- Living rent free or at a discounted rate in P's property (even if it is on the basis that they are caring for P).
- Selling P's home to someone else at an undervalue (regardless of whether the buyer is a close family member who is purchasing the property to release cash to fund P's needs).
- Giving someone an interest-free loan from P's funds (regardless of whether the loan is to give a loved one some immediate relief with a view that the loan will be repaid to P during P's lifetime).

In each of the above examples, the transaction will fall under the definition of a "gift" since it will inadvertently result in P's estate being depleted either in an active way (for instance, P's bank balance being reduced by paying school fees) or in a passive way (for instance, by not receiving rental income or interest payment which P may otherwise be entitled to).

An attorney or deputy should be cautious when they consider making gifts of such nature. They owe a fiduciary duty to P and once they take control of P's property and affairs, they are not authorised to dispose of P's assets even if their intention is to do the "right" thing. To manage this risk, the Mental Capacity Act 2005 sets out in clear terms the circumstances in which an attorney or a deputy can make gifts on behalf of P without breaching their fiduciary duty or being in a position of conflict with P.

3.2 – The statutory power of an an EPA attorney[35] to gift

This is set out clearly in paragraph 3(3) of Schedule 4 of the Mental Capacity Act 2005:

> "*...an attorney under an enduring power, whether general or limited, may (without obtaining any consent) dispose of the property of the donor by way of gift to the following extent but no further –*
>
> *(a) he may make gifts of a seasonal nature or at a time, or on an anniversary, of a birth, a marriage or the formation of a civil partnership, to persons (including himself) who are related to or connected to the donor, and*
>
> *(b) he may make gifts to any charity to whom the donor made or might be expected to make gifts,*
>
> *provided that the value of each gift is not unreasonable having regard to all the circumstances and in particular the size of the donor's estate.*"

3.3 – The statutory power of an LPA attorney[36] to gift

A similar authority is given to attorneys acting under a Lasting Power of Attorney in section 12(2) of the Mental Capacity Act 2005 which states that:

> "*The donee may make gifts –*
>
> *(a) on customary occasions to persons (including himself) who are related to or connected with the donor, or*

---

35 An attorney who has been appointed by virtue of an Enduring Power of Attorney instrument.

36 An attorney who has been appointed by virtue of a Lasting Power of Attorney instrument.

(b) to any charity to whom the donor made or might have been expected to make gifts

if the value of each such gift is not unreasonable having regard to all the circumstances and, in particular, the size of the donor's estate."

3.4 – The power of a deputy[37] to gift

The scope of a deputy's authority to gift is usually set out in the Deputyship Order made by the Court of Protection in the following standard paragraph:

> "*The deputies may (without obtaining any further authority from the court) dispose of P's money or property by way of gift to any charity to which P made, or might have been expected to make, such gifts, and, on customary occasions, to persons who are related to or connected with P, provided that the value of each such gift is not unreasonable having regard to all circumstances and, in particular, the size of P's estate.*"

37 Someone appointed by the Court of Protection to manage P's property and affairs.

Author's note – Gifting can be important to maintain relationships with close family members and friends. This is recognised by the law, hence attorneys and deputies are given some power to gift on behalf of P as set out above. However, it is also recognised that this power can be misused which is why there are restrictions in place. Attorneys and deputies should respect these restrictions and carefully consider the following before making a gift:

- for what occasion the gift is being made;
- is the recipient of the gift connected to P;
- whether the gift is affordable given the value of P's estate;
- whether it is reasonable to make the gift.

The author deals with further factors which attorneys and deputies must have regard to in Chapter 4.

3.5 – Gifting or maintenance?

Making maintenance payments is different to making a gift on behalf of P. One of the defining features of maintenance payments is its regularity to meet the ongoing needs of family members and dependants – for instance, payments being made on a weekly or monthly basis. Gifts, on the other hand, often lack regularity and are made for a special occasion or to meet a specific need.

Providing for the needs of another person is not uncommon. There are many instances when one will assume financial responsibility for someone else and make regular payments to them – such as a spouse who has historically been the main breadwinner and supports their family; a parent helping a child who is struggling financially with their living costs; or a grandparent paying for a grandchild's school fees.

Someone who has the relevant capacity can decide who they wish to help financially and maintain during their lifetime. However, the situation changes when that person loses the capacity to make such decisions and becomes "P". The question then arises as to whether P's attorney or deputy can continue making the regular maintenance payments. The matter is further complicated if the attorney or deputy is also the person being maintained by P. As a reminder, the primary duty of an attorney or a deputy is to act in P's best interests and they owe a fiduciary duty to P. They should neither gain any personal benefit from their position nor should they place themselves in a position of conflict where their personal interests (or the interests of a person they are connect to) conflict with P's interests.

The law recognises the financial obligation which some individuals may have towards others. It is therefore possible for attorneys and deputies to make maintenance payments to others using P's funds. However, as with the making of gifts, there are limits imposed and it is important for the attorney or deputy to check the Power of Attorney instrument or the Deputyship Order in the first instance. This is because the law draws a distinction between a deputy[38] and an EPA attorney[39] on the one hand and an LPA attorney[40] on the other hand.

3.6 – Maintenance payments made by a deputy or an EPA attorney

The Court of Protection will usually give express permission to a deputy to make provisions for the needs of someone related or connected to P. This specific authority will normally form part of a standard Deputyship

38 Someone appointed by the Court of Protection to manage P's property and affairs.

39 An attorney who has been appointed by virtue of an Enduring Power of Attorney instrument.

40 An attorney who has been appointed by virtue of a Lasting Power of Attorney instrument.

Order and readers are advised to check whether the following wording is included:

> *"The deputy may make provisions for the needs of anyone who is related to or connected with P if he provided for, or might be expected to provide for that person's needs by doing whatever he did, or might reasonably be expected to do, to meet those needs."*

Similarly, the Mental Capacity Act 2005[41] makes provisions for attorneys acting under an Enduring Power of Attorney to make maintenance payments:

> *"Subject to any conditions or restrictions contained in the instrument, an attorney under an enduring power, whether general or limited, may (without obtaining any consent) act under the power so as to benefit himself or other persons than the donor to the following extent but no further –*
>
> *(a) he may so act in relation to himself or in relation to any person if the donor might be expected to provide for his or that person's needs respectively, and*
>
> *(b) he may do whatever the donor might be expected to do to meet those needs."*

Since express permission is granted to a deputy or an EPA attorney, they are not obliged to make an application seeking the Court of Protection's approval to make maintenance payments. However, they should not mistake this express permission for complete freedom to maintain someone else at the expense of P. P's best interests should remain at the forefront of their mind.

41 Mental Capacity Act 2005, Schedule 4, Part 1, para 3(2).

Author's note – Before making maintenance payments to themselves or someone else, a deputy or an EPA attorney should:[42]

- check the wording of the Deputyship Order or the Enduring Power of Attorney instrument to make sure there are no restrictions in respect of maintenance payments.
- ensure the maintenance payments are being made to someone P historically provided for or might be expected to provide for.
- more importantly, ensure that paying out maintenance will not have an adverse impact on P's financial welfare.
- go through the best-interests checklist (see Chapter 6) and keep a record of their reasoning behind making such payments.

If in doubt, seek legal advice and/or guidance from the Office of the Public Guardian.

3.7 – Maintenance payments made by an LPA attorney

The Mental Capacity Act 2005 does not grant express permission to an LPA attorney to make maintenance payments to others using P's funds. The position of an LPA attorney is therefore different from that of a deputy or an EPA attorney – it can be onerous when it comes to maintenance payments.

This is why it is advisable for donors to include a clear and explicit condition or statement in their Lasting Power of Attorney instrument for their attorney to meet the needs of specific persons. This would give the LPA attorney some level of protection. However, this may also place the attorney in a position of conflict and there have been cases where

42 This is not intended to be an exhaustive list and other factors should also be considered depending on P's circumstances.

attempts made by the donor of a Lasting Power of Attorney to extend their attorney's power to maintain someone have been rejected. For example, in the case of **Re Wheatley (2011)**[43], the donor had made the following provision in their Lasting Power of Attorney:

> *"My attorneys will continue to make contributions to my grandchildren's Child Trust Funds and any other saving/pension plans that I fund for their benefit."*

The Public Guardian made an application to the Court of Protection seeking to sever this provision prior to the registration of the Lasting Power of Attorney. In their view, the provision contravened section 12 of the Mental Capacity Act 2005 which places restrictions on an attorney's authority to make gifts. The Public Guardian's application was successful and as a result, the attorney could not rely on this provision to continue making contributions to P's grandchildren.

LPA attorneys, however, have general powers to deal with P's property and affairs under section 9 of the Mental Capacity Act 2005.[44] Arguably, this general power can extend to meeting the needs of someone who P was in the habit of maintaining. Nonetheless, attorneys should go through the decision-making process set out in Chapter 6 and consider whether continuing with the maintenance payments is in P's best interests.

---

43 Re Wheatley (2011) COP 31/1/11.

44 Mental capacity Act 2005, section 9(1)(b).

Author's note – LPA attorneys should be prudent and, if appropriate, seek the Court of Protection's approval before continuing with P's historical habit of paying maintenance. The Court of Protection is likely to be understanding where maintenance payments are required to meet the needs of P's spouse, partner or a dependant child given P's legal obligation to meet their needs. An LPA attorney may find it helpful to seek guidance from the Office of the Public Guardian in the first instance before making an application to the Court of Protection.

CHAPTER FOUR

WHAT TO CONSIDER WHEN MAKING AN AUTHORISED GIFT?

An attorney or a deputy can use P's funds or assets to make a gift to themselves or others provided the gift is given to someone who is connected to P or to a charity P would have normally given to; is being made on a customary occasion or is of a seasonal nature; and is reasonable in value, given the size of P's estate and their expected future needs.

In a nutshell, attorneys and deputies have sufficient powers to make gifts in certain circumstances, making it an "authorised" gift. However, they are not obligated to make a gift on behalf of P and should not allow others to pressure them into it. Simply because a gift is authorised does not necessarily mean that it should be made without the attorney or the deputy giving the matter further consideration.

Attorneys and deputies are reminded that their primary obligation is to P. They should therefore carefully assess whether the proposed gift is affordable and in P's best interests. The next section addresses the factors which attorneys and deputies should have regard to.

4.1 – Factors to consider before making an authorised gift

A helpful guide as to what additional factors attorneys and deputies should consider before making a financial decision on behalf of P is set out in the case of **Re Buckley [2013]**.[45] Although a large part of the

45 Re Buckley: The Public Guardian v C [2013] EWHC 2965

judgment in this case relates to the investment made using P's funds, it is of relevance as it lists important factors which attorneys and deputies should consider when parting with P's funds.

In the case of **Re Buckley**, the Office of the Public Guardian received a complaint in respect of the manner in which P's niece and attorney was managing P's finances. They carried out a formal investigation and discovered several suspicious dealings which included the withdrawal of the sum of £72,000 by the attorney to set up a reptile breeding business and she had made gifts in the sum of at least £7,650 to herself. The Office of the Public Guardian were concerned that P's estate may have incurred a total loss of approximately £150,000. An application was subsequently made by the Public Guardian for the Court to revoke the Lasting Power of Attorney.

It was the attorney's position that she invested in the reptile breeding business since P "*loves animals and I felt that this would be an investment she would be happy about.*"[46] In respect of the monies the attorney used for her personal benefit, her response was that the money was used with P's permission and "*She has given me money in the past and this was not unusual for her as we were very close.*"[47]

The application came before Senior Judge Lush who considered the evidence and reminded the parties that attorneys hold a fiduciary position which imposes a number of duties on them.[48] The Court ultimately found that the attorney had breached her fiduciary duty by investing P's funds in her own business; contravened her authority by using the sum of £43,317.47 for her own benefit; and acted in a way that was not in P's best interests. As a result, the Lasting Power of Attorney was revoked.

---

46 Re Buckley: The Public Guardian v C [2013] EWHC 2965, para 15.

47 Re Buckley: The Public Guardian v C [2013] EWHC 2965, paragraph 18.

48 Re Buckley: The Public Guardian v C [2013] EWHC 2965, paragraph 25.

In his judgment, Senior Judge Lush referred to a guide on "Investing for Patients".[49] Although the guide is specific to investments, it lists several factors which should be considered when parting with P's funds and the author sets out below a few of these factors:[50]

- P's age.
- P's life expectancy and whether there is reason to believe that P's state of health is life-threatening.
- Whether the proposed gift is to be paid from P's capital which generates an income for P.
- Whether the gift will consequentially affect P's current and future income.
- Whether any major items of expenditure are anticipated or should be planned for.
- Whether any gifts or payments to dependants are likely to be made.
- The interests of beneficiaries under P's Will or intestacy.

4.2 – Case Study (Part 1): An attorney's quandary

Let's consider a scenario where P has a history of giving expensive Christmas and birthday presents.

---

49 Senior Judge Lush quoted suggestions from the guidance "*Investing for Patients*" issued to the Court of Protection and the Office of the Public Guardian staff prior to the Mental Capacity Act 2005 coming into effect.

50 This is not intended to be an exhaustive list.

Derek was a successful professional working in the banking sector. He earned a good wage and has always been generous to his nephews and nieces. He would regularly send them money including a cheque for £500 to each of his 8 nephews and nieces at Christmas and on birthdays. His nephews and nieces are also the beneficiaries of his estate.

Derek is unmarried, has no children and lives on his own. Sadly, 5 years ago, at the age of 50, Derek developed early onset of dementia. He was initially able to manage on his own. He carried on working and seeing his nephews and nieces and gifted them the same amount (£500) at Christmas and on birthdays. Recently, his condition has deteriorated to the point that he is no longer able to work and live on his own. Derek had always expressed a wish to remain in his own home for as long as he can. He owns his property outright (valued at £500,000) and has savings, stocks and shares valued at £200,000. Derek now requires 24hr live-in carers and if he is to remain in his own home, the estimated monthly cost of carers will be £10,000 (approximately £120,000 a year).

John is Derek's registered LPA attorney. He is a good friend of Derek and has a close relationship with Derek's nephews and nieces. In fact, Derek often gifted John monies at Christmas. John has recently taken over the management of Derek's finances after he was assessed as lacking the capacity to manage his property and affairs. It is January and Derek's nephews and nieces have been in contact with John, asking why they have not received their yearly Christmas present from their uncle Derek.

John would like to keep making gifts in line with Derek's known gifting habit. However, he is also aware that Derek's cash assets will start depleting if 24hr live-in carers are employed and he will run out of funds within a couple of years. John is under a lot of pressure from Derek's nephews and nieces and is concerned that they will become hostile towards him and Derek if gifts are not made. He is in a quandary and seeks your advice on whether he should continue making gifts on behalf of Derek.

A good starting point for an attorney or a deputy is to check whether the proposed gift is lawful under the Mental Capacity Act 2005 or in the Deputyship Order. In this case study, the gifts which John is considering making are for a customary occasion. They are therefore authorised pursuant to section12(2) of the Mental Capacity Act 2005 and John is likely to form the view that since this is something which Derek was in the habit of doing, there is no harm in carrying on with it.

However, this is not the end of the matter. As mentioned above, it is not sufficient for John to consider only these two factors: – 1) whether the gifts are lawful and 2) whether they are in line with Derek's gifting habit?

Whereas John may have the statutory authority to make the gifts, he should be advised that an authorised gift should only be made when it is of a *reasonable value* and does not adversely affect *P's interests.* John should therefore consider other factors and not allow Derek's nephews and nieces to pressure him into parting with Derek's funds.

4.3 – Case study (Part 2): P's best interests

Derek's health and financial situation have clearly changed of late. John, in his capacity as Derek's attorney, is now responsible for managing Derek's finances. He is accountable for the decisions he makes and ultimately, should act in Derek's best interests.

Continuing with the same pattern of gifting is not likely to be in Derek's best interests for several reasons including:

- Derek is only 50 years old and is likely to live for several years.
- His medical condition is progressive and is likely to deteriorate.
- Derek's care needs are therefore likely to increase.

- Derek has expressed a wish, at a time when he had capacity, that he would like to remain in his own home and John should try and respect this wish.

- Respecting Derek's wish will mean spending around £10,000 a month which is likely to increase over time.

- Whilst Derek has £200,000 which can be converted into cash assets, this will soon be depleted as a result of his care costs.

It is clear from the above that gifting £500 to each and every of the 8 nephews and nieces twice a year, at Christmas and on birthdays (£8,000 in total per year), may no longer be affordable for Derek if he is to remain living in his home for as long as possible.

Before making a decision, John should be advised to collate and assess the following:[51]

- An updated valuation of Derek's assets.

- A report from an appropriate expert to have a better understanding of what Derek's current and future medical and social needs are likely to be.

- Quantify the costs of Derek's current and future needs.

- Seek financial advice on whether Derek's capital should be invested to generate an income to meet his current and future needs at home for a longer period of time.

51 This is not intended to be an exhaustive list. Each case will turn on its facts.

- Look at Derek's Will to see if the gifts are likely to affect Derek's testamentary wishes.

After considering the above, John is likely to come to the conclusion that making large gifts should cease. However, this does not mean that gifts should not be made at all. John may form the view that whilst gifting at the same level is no longer affordable, gifting a smaller amount only once a year is an expense which Derek's estate can afford and will preserve Derek's relationship with his nephews and nieces.[52] Ultimately, John should be advised that he should not make financial decisions which will have an adverse effect on Derek's current and future quality of life – even if this means disappointing Derek's nephews and neices whom he has a good relationship with. John should also be advised not to place himself in a position of conflict and reconsider the gift which he used to receive from Derek at Christmas.

52 It would be prudent for John to keep a record of his reasoning for making gifts of a smaller value and the status of Derek's finances at the time.

CHAPTER FIVE

UNAUTHORISED GIFTS

Attorneys and deputies are reminded that they should not make gifts which do not fall within the scope of their powers. Gifting is one of the clearest ways in which their power can be misused (whether intentionally or not) and restrictions have been put in place to prevent them from taking advantage of their position, especially if the attorney or deputy has fallen on hard times and has almost convinced themselves that P would have wanted them to benefit. If a proposed gift falls outside the scope of their powers, they should seek the Court of Protection's approval in the first instance by making an application pursuant to section 18(1)(b) or section 23(4)[53] of the Mental Capacity Act 2005.

5.1 – Common misconceptions

Practitioners will have no doubt come across clients who, unbeknown to them, have made unauthorised gifts. Very often, their intention is simply to help people connected to P. The author lists below common reasons often given by attorneys and deputies when justifying why an unauthorised gift was made to themselves or others:

- *"[P] had capacity and said that I could have the money."*
- *"[P] would have wanted me to have the money if only they had capacity."*
- *"It will all be mine soon anyway, so what is the problem?"*

53 This applies to attorneys acting under a Lasting Power of Attorney.

- *"I deserve this, for all the sacrifice I am making."*
- *"I will return the money, if [P] ever has a need for it."*
- *"If [P] does not mind and is well cared for, what is the harm?"*[54]

Attorneys and deputies sometimes abuse their position because of a lack of awareness or understanding of the extent of their powers. However, this is not a valid justification for their action. This was made very clear by Senior Judge Lush in the case of **Re Buckley: The Public Guardian v C [2013]**[55] who reminded attorneys that they should be aware of the law regarding their role and responsibilities and "*Ignorance is no excuse.*"[56]

5.2 – Case Study

Let's consider a scenario involving an unauthorised gift. As mentioned in Chapter 3, a gift is not simply the transfer of money. It can take several shapes and forms, such as using P's money to purchase a property in someone else's name.

> *Peter and Doris were married for over 50 years and had 4 children. Doris died three years ago and soon after her death, Peter's behaviour started changing. The children initially thought that the change was a result of their father mourning the death of their mother. Sadly, 3 of Peter's children stopped visiting him after Doris died. Peter found this hurtful and a few months after Doris' death, he saw a solicitor and changed his Will to*

54 This specific response was given by the attorney to the OPG's investigating officer. See the case of Re EG [2015] EWCOP 6, para 10.

55 Re Buckley: The Public Guardian v C [2013] EWHC 2965 (COP).

56 Re Buckley: The Public Guardian v C [2013] EWHC 2965 (COP), para 44.

appoint his youngest child, Graham, as his sole beneficiary since Graham remained in contact with him and supported him.

Two years ago, Peter's doctor diagnosed him with dementia. Nonetheless Peter, who is retired, remained capable of handling his finances and managing on his own at home. Peter's main asset is the family home valued at £250,000 and his monthly income consists of his state pension.

Last year, Peter started struggling to manage on his own. He would leave the kettle on and wander in the streets. Peter had previously made a Lasting Power of Attorney appointing Doris and Graham as his property and affairs attorneys on a joint and several basis[57]*. Graham remained Peter's attorney after Doris' death and an application to appoint a deputy to manage Peter's finances was not required.*

It became obvious that Peter could no longer live in the family home on his own. He became paranoid and would not seek help from anyone but Graham. He subsequently moved in with Graham. Graham was a small business owner. The plan was for Graham's wife to look after Peter. Sadly, Graham's wife could not deal with the pressure of looking after an elderly person and left Graham. Graham struggled to keep his business going whilst caring for Peter. His business folded a few months ago. Graham started looking after Peter on a full-time basis.

Since Peter no longer lived in the family home, Graham arranged for it to be sold in his capacity as Peter's attorney. Graham needed an income to support himself and Peter and pay his own mortgage. Upon selling the family home, Graham used the sale proceeds and purchased an investment property in his sole name from which he drew a rental income.

Graham's 3 siblings have become aware that the family home has been sold and have asked Graham for an explanation. Graham did not respond and the siblings reported their concerns to the Office of the Public Guardian.

57 Attorneys can be appointed jointly (which means decisions need to be made unanimously) or jointly and severally (which means that they can make decisions independently of one another).

The Office of the Public Guardian has been in contact with Graham and are carrying out an investigation. Graham now seeks your advice. He informs you that the sale proceeds were a gift made by Peter for the sacrifices Graham made which caused his marriage to break down and business to fold. Peter knew what he was doing at the time.

In Graham's view, Peter is comfortable and well looked after by a family member in a familiar environment. The alternative, as Graham saw it, was either (i) for Peter to have several carers visiting the family home to check on him which Peter would find very unsettling given the paranoia he had developed and which he would struggle to afford; or (ii) for Peter to sell the family home, move into a care home and use the sale proceeds to fund his care. Peter and Doris had both mentioned to Graham in the past that they did not want to move into a care home in their old age and Graham wanted to respect Peter's wish.

Graham is adamant that the steps he took were to help Peter. His siblings have not done anything to help their father. The sale proceeds of the family home have been invested in a buy-to-let property and the rental income is funding Peter's lifestyle. Graham makes sure that all of Peter's needs are met. According to him, ultimately, whatever is left after Peter dies would go to him by virtue of Peter's Will. He therefore does not see any harm in what he has done.

Graham should be advised that even though his intention was to help Peter, in the eyes of the law, using the sale proceeds of the family home to purchase an investment property in Graham's sole name may not be lawful and is likely to be challenged for numerous reasons, the main ones being:

- Peter may not have had the necessary capacity to gift the sale proceeds to Graham when the family home was sold.
- Peter did not receive any legal advice to understand the implications of making this gift to Graham.

- The gift which Graham made in his capacity as Peter's attorney was not for a customary occasion and was therefore unauthorised.

- The gift is not reasonable in value or affordable given that it was Peter's main asset.

- Graham has denied Peter of all his capital during his lifetime. Peter only has his state pension as an income and he has no reserve to meet any unforeseen expenses.

Even though Peter is well cared for and his needs are being adequately met, Graham has breached his fiduciary duty by selling the property in his capacity as Peter's attorney and appropriating the sale proceeds in his sole name. He has not acted in Peter's best interests by depleting his estate during his lifetime and the Public Guardian will expect him to restore Peter's estate by paying an amount equivalent to the net sale proceeds of the family home into Peter's account or by potentially transferring the legal and beneficial interest in the investment property into Peter's name and to account for the rental income. It matters not that Graham will ultimately receive Peter's estate after Peter's death.

Graham should be advised that if he does not restore Peter's estate, he is at risk of being removed as Peter's attorney and court proceedings may be brought against him.[58] However, given that Graham is Peter's full-time carer and Peter is living in Graham's property, he should also be advised to consider making an application seeking the Court of Protection's approval to receive gratuitous care payments as well as a contribution towards his household expenses from Peter. In taking these

58 See Chapter 11.4 and 11.6 in which the author addresses the consequences of not seeking the Court of Protection's approval to make an unauthorised gift. There is also a potential claim to challenge the lifetime gift and that presumed undue influence took place given that Graham acted in his capacity as Peter's attorney.

steps, Peter's interests as well as Graham's interests could potentially be lawfully preserved.

5.3 – De minimis principle

The law is strict when it comes to the limited circumstances in which an attorney or a deputy can make gifts on P's behalf. But it is also recognised that gifts are not given only on customary occasions and gifts are often made on an ad hoc basis – for instance, a grandparent giving some money to a grandchild when they visit or when a close family member or a friend is struggling financially one particular month. Due to the nature of these gifts not being "customary" or of a "seasonal nature" (and are therefore unauthorised), an attorney or a deputy should not make them without seeking the Court of Protection's approval.

However, very often, the gifts mentioned above are not substantial. In such circumstances, is it in P's interests to incur the costs of a formal application to the Court of Protection to approve a small gift because it is not authorised by law?

This was addressed by Senior Judge Lush in the case of **GM, MJ and JM [2013]**.[59] In this case, Senior Judge Lush highlighted that there may be circumstances where the potential infringement is so minor that it would be disproportionate to make a formal application to the court,[60] referring to the de minimis exception. De minimis applies in cases where an attorney or a deputy finds themselves in a position where small gifts are found to be appropriate but fall outside the scope of their powers. If applications were to be made for each and every one of these gifts, the Court of Protection would not only be overwhelmed with applications, but the level of gift involved would not justify the legal costs involved.

59 GM, MJ and JM [2013] COPLR 290.

60 GM, MJ and JM [2013] COPLR 290, para 43.

The de minimis principle should therefore be considered when advising attorneys and deputies on a proposed gift. This principle allows them to make gifts totalling £5,500 in one year: covering the annual IHT exemption of £3,000 plus an annual small gift exemption of £250 per person, up to maximum of 10 people (that is, another £2,500). However, attorneys and deputies should also be aware that the de minimis exception can only be applied in the following limited circumstances:

- P has a life expectancy of less than 5 years.
- P's estate exceeds the nil rate band for inheritance tax purposes (currently £325,000).[61]
- The gifts are affordable and will not have an adverse impact on P's standard of care and quality of life.
- There is no evidence that P would be opposed to gifts of this level being made on their behalf.

Gifts made under the de minimis principle would not be deemed unlawful provided the above conditions are met. Attorneys and deputies are advised to keep a clear record of their reasoning behind the gifts as well as P's financial circumstances at the time.

5.4 – Inheritance tax planning

With estates growing in value, it is not unusual for attorneys and deputies to seek financial advice on the management of P's estate, particularly when the value of the estate exceeds the nil rate band for inheritance tax.[62] Tax planning forms part of this advice. There may be circumstances when attorneys and deputies are advised by other professionals to make

61 Information stands correct as of November 2023.

62 £325,000 as of November 2023.

gifts which will result in some form of financial or tax benefit to P's estate. However, gifting for the purposes of mitigating tax is not within the scope of an attorney's or a deputy's powers and is therefore unauthorised. The Court of Protection's approval will be required.

As already mentioned, any decision made by an attorney or a deputy must be in P's best interests. From this standpoint, gifting for the purposes of reducing inheritance tax payable by P's beneficiaries after P's death will not be of any direct benefit to P. If anything, such gifts will reduce the capital available to P during their lifetime. This raises the question whether there is any merit in making an application for the purposes of inheritance tax planning given that P would not have any direct benefit.

There are no set provisions on matters relating to inheritance tax planning in the Mental Capacity Act 2005. Such an application will be case and fact specific and there are reported cases from which guidance can be sought.

In the case of **Re JDS; KGS v JDS [2012]**[63], P, a young man received an amount in excess of £2m in damages for clinical damages. He was an only child who lived with his parents. An application was made by P's deputy (a professional deputy) to make gifts to the value of £500,000[64] to P's parents for the purposes of reducing the amount of inheritance tax they would have to pay upon P's death. The application was dismissed. Whilst Senior Judge Lush acknowledged that the Court is generally sympathetic towards family members who take on a caring role and dedicate their lives to looking after P, he commented that it is not the function of the Court of Protection to maximise any potential inheritance for the benefit

63 KGS v JDS [2012] EWCOP 302 (19 January 2012).

64 This is an example showing that gifts can take several shapes and forms. In this case, it was the transfer of equity to the value of £500,000 in P's family home to his parents.

of family members on P's death, because this was not the purpose for which the personal injury compensation was awarded.[65]

However, the facts were different in the case of **PBC v JMA and others [2018]**[66] and the author strongly recommends that practitioners review and consider this judgment before advising clients on making an application to the Court of Protection.

The above-mentioned case also involved the gifting of P's monies for inheritance tax planning. P was a 72-year old woman who had been diagnosed with dementia. Her son was appointed as her sole attorney with authority to manage her property and affairs. P's estate was estimated to be £18m and consisted mainly of investments and shares. The attorney made an application seeking the Court of Protection's approval to make various gifts exceeding £7m to himself and various charities. His application stated at section 5.3 of form COP1 "*... if the following gifts were made now and [JMA] were to survive at least a further three years, then there would be significant inheritance tax savings on her death.*"[67]

P was joined as a party to the proceedings and the Official Solicitor was appointed to represent her. An agreement was reached by all the parties in the proceedings in respect of the attorney's proposed gifts. Interestingly, despite having an agreement in place, the matter was listed for an attended hearing. The Judge wished to understand in what sense the proposed gifts were for P's benefit and to what extent the proposed gifts were in accordance with P's past and present wishes, feelings, values and beliefs.

This judgment is of particular importance since it sets out how the Judge conducted a balancing exercise before concluding that the factors

65 KGS v JDS [2012] EWCOP 302, para 39.

66 PBC v JMA and others [2018] EWCOP 19 (16 April 2018).

67 PBC v JMA and others [2018] EWCOP 19, para 5.

weighed in favour of the application. She also made it clear in her judgment that the Mental Capacity Act 2005 does not permit the Court to rely on "default positions, assumptions or generalisations" that most people would engage in tax planning. The Court of Protection will consider the factors set out in section 4 of the Mental Capacity Act 2005 and the facts in the particular case.[68]

The author lists below the key relevant factors which the Judge had regard to: [69]

- P's past wishes and feelings: The Judge noted that P clearly wanted her son and the charities to benefit. This was evidenced by the various gifts P made to them in the past as well as the wishes she expressed in her Will – which left her residuary estate to her son as well as pecuniary gifts to the charities.

- P's habit of seeking tax advice: The Judge found that when P had capacity, she regularly sought advice from experts when she could, particularly to minimise her exposure to lifetime taxes.

- P's financial welfare: P's estate was large and the proposed gifts amounted to only 38% of her estate. There would be sufficient funds to meet P's financial needs during her lifetime and the gifts were therefore affordable.

- Family relationship: the Judge considered the relationship P has with her family and concluded that giving effect to the agreement reached by the parties would avoid any further argument and have a beneficial effect on family relations.

---

68 PBC v JMA and others [2018] EWCOP 19, para 66.

69 PBC v JMA and others [2018] EWCOP 19, para 67. See the table weighing the factors in favour of and against the making of the proposed gifts.

Author's note – Tax planning, on its own, is not sufficient to convince the Court of the Protection that a proposed gift should be approved. P's finances, age, health, family dynamics and testamentary wishes are a few of the factors which the Court will have regard to. In the case of PBC v JMA and others [2018], had P been younger with a longer life expectancy and limited funds, it is sensible to assume that the Court of Protection would not have approved the gifts purely to reduce the inheritance tax payable after her death.

CHAPTER SIX

DECISION-MAKING PROCESS

There are instances when the making of an unauthorised gift may be appropriate or justified– for instance, when a family member has an immediate need to pay for private medical treatment; to provide for a close family member or a friend from surplus capital which P has received from winning the lottery or by inheriting from someone else's estate; or for inheritance tax planning, depending on the facts of the case.[70]

However, even if appropriate and justified, these gifts remain unauthorised and attorneys and deputies should seek the Court of Protection's approval. Prior to making an application to the Court of Protection, it is important to go through a decision-making process to assess whether the proposed gift is in P's best interests and the Court of Protection is likely to approve it. The focus of this Chapter is on section 4 of the Mental Capacity Act 2005 and it addresses the checklist which a decision-maker as well as the Court of Protection must have regard to when dealing with P's finances.

6.1 – Best interests checklist

Readers are reminded of the primary message of the Mental Capacity Act 2005: any decision made should be in *P's best interests*. This is the overarching principle. However, the Mental Capacity Act 2005 does not give a specific definition of "*best interests*". Instead, in section 4, it sets

70 See Chapter 5.4 on inheritance tax planning.

out a checklist and a process to follow when making decisions quoted in the following:

> *(1) In determining for the purposes of this Act what is in a person's best interests, the person making the determination must not make it merely on the basis of—*
>
> > *(a) the person's age or appearance, or*
> >
> > *(b) a condition of his, or an aspect of his behaviour, which might lead others to make unjustified assumptions about what might be in his best interests.*
>
> *(2) The person making the determination must consider all the relevant circumstances and, in particular, take the following steps.*
>
> *(3) He must consider—*
>
> > *(a) whether it is likely that the person will at some time have capacity in relation to the matter in question, and*
> >
> > *(b) if it appears likely that he will, when that is likely to be.*
>
> *(4) He must, so far as reasonably practicable, permit and encourage the person to participate, or to improve his ability to participate, as fully as possible in any act done for him and any decision affecting him.*
>
> *(5) Where the determination relates to life-sustaining treatment he must not, in considering whether the treatment is in the best interests of the person concerned, be motivated by a desire to bring about his death.*
>
> *(6) He must consider, so far as is reasonably ascertainable—*

(a) the person's past and present wishes and feelings (and, in particular, any relevant written statement made by him when he had capacity),

(b) the beliefs and values that would be likely to influence his decision if he had capacity, and

(c) the other factors that he would be likely to consider if he were able to do so.

(7) He must take into account, if it is practicable and appropriate to consult them, the views of—

(a) anyone named by the person as someone to be consulted on the matter in question or on matters of that kind,

(b) anyone engaged in caring for the person or interested in his welfare,

(c) any donee of a lasting power of attorney granted by the person, and

(d) any deputy appointed for the person by the court,

as to what would be in the person's best interests and, in particular, as to the matters mentioned in subsection (6).

(8) The duties imposed by subsections (1) to (7) also apply in relation to the exercise of any powers which—

(a) are exercisable under a lasting power of attorney, or

(b) are exercisable by a person under this Act where he reasonably believes that another person lacks capacity.

(9) In the case of an act done, or a decision made, by a person other than the court, there is sufficient compliance with this section if

(having complied with the requirements of subsections (1) to (7)) he reasonably believes that what he does or decides is in the best interests of the person concerned.

(10) "Life-sustaining treatment" means treatment which in the view of a person providing health care for the person concerned is necessary to sustain life.

(11) "Relevant circumstances" are those—

(a) of which the person making the determination is aware, and

(b) which it would be reasonable to regard as relevant.

It is important for any practitioner preparing an application to address the above in their application and put forward relevant evidence to show how the proposed gift in question will benefit P.

6.2 – P's wishes and feelings: the subjective or objective test?

Part of the process in determining whether a particular decision is in P's best interests is to consider P's past and present wishes and feelings as set out in section 4(6)(a) of the Mental Capacity Act 2005.

Given that P may no longer have the capacity to make the specific decision in question and therefore express their views (hence the need to make an application to the Court of Protection), how would the Court of Protection determine what P's present wishes, feelings, beliefs and values are in line with section 4(6)(a)-(b) of the Mental Capacity Act 2005?

Prior to the Mental Capacity Act 2005, the "*substituted judgment*" approach was adopted by the Court. The Court would, in effect, place themselves in the shoes of P and ask the question "*What might P be expected to have done?*". The Court would then make a decision based on what P, acting reasonably, would have made for himself. However, the Court of Protection now adopts a different approach. Its approach is more objective with a view to determining what is in P's best interests as opposed to what P might have expected to have done. This is because what is in P's best interests *is not necessarily the same as doing what P would have wanted to do.*

Very often, excessive emphasis is placed by the applicant on what P would have done if they had capacity. The Court of Protection will no doubt consider this factor but will also adopt a balance sheet approach overall: it will weigh up all the relevant factors before reaching a conclusion on what is in P's best interests.[71] This does not mean that P's wishes, feelings, beliefs and values will not be considered. Caselaw shows that these will remain a significant factor and there will inadvertently be an element of substituted judgment when going through the decision-making process. However, they will not be determinative since other factors will also be considered.

This was addressed by Mr Justice Morgan in the case of **Re G (TJ) [2010]**.[72] An application was made by a deputy seeking the Court's authority to continue making payments of £3,300 a month to P's daughter from P's surplus funds. The application (which was not contested by any of the parties) was made on the basis that the proposed payments would be what P would have wanted if she had the capacity to make the decision for herself, which in effect, was applying a "substituted judgment". The Judge confirmed that whilst section 4 of the Mental Capacity Act 2005 requires the decision-maker to consider several factors and apply an objective test, he also acknowledged this would involve an element of substituted judgment being taken into account pursuant to section (4)(6)(b) and (c) of the Mental Capacity Act 2005 which refers

---

71 There is not a hierarchy in respect of the factors listed in section 4. Each case will turn on its facts. A factor of magnetic importance in one case may not carry the same weight in another case.

72 Re G(TJ) [2010] EWHC 3005 (COP).

to the beliefs and values which would be likely to consider if P were able to make the relevant decision.[73] However, it was made clear that the ultimate test for the court is an objective test and that *"A substituted judgment can be subsumed into the consideration of best interests."*[74]

6.3 – The process to follow

The checklist set out in section 4 of the Mental Capacity Act is the starting point when one considers making a best-interests decision or an application to the Court of Protection. In addition to P's wishes, feelings, beliefs and values, it is important to have regard to the following matters:

- Ensure that pre-conceived conclusions or assumptions have not been drawn purely on P's age, appearance and medical condition.[75]
- The likelihood of P regaining capacity to make certain decisions and when that is likely to be.[76]
- Encourage P to participate in making the decision in question.[77]
- Seek the views of others engaged or interested in P's welfare.

73 Re G(TJ) [2010] EWHC 3005 (COP), para 36.

74 Re G(TJ) [2010] EWHC 3005 (COP), para 65.

75 See Chapter 1.4 for general assumptions which can easily be made following the diagnosis of a medical condition.

76 Unless time is of the essence, P should be encouraged to make the decision himself. Making a premature application would not be in P's best interests.

77 This may involve using specific tools, sign language or discussing matters with P when they are likely to be more alert and engaged.

- Seek the views of P's attorney or deputy.

- List the relevant factors which the decision-maker is aware of which would have a bearing on the decision which needs to be made.

A relevant factor to consider is the emotional and social impact the proposed gift will have – not only on P but on those whom P relies on. An example is the case of **David Ross v A [2015]**[78] which involved P who had received a lump sum payment of £5m upon the conclusion of a medical negligence claim. Payments were made by P's deputy to fund P's brother's school fees; changes made to the family home to meet P's needs; the purchase of a holiday home and payments to maintain the family home since P's parents had stopped working to care for P. An application was made by the deputy seeking the Court's approval to pay P's brother's school fees. Arguments were advanced by the Official Solicitor representing P that the lump sum paid to P from the medical negligence claim was for P's benefit and not for the benefit of her family members; and that P had a long life expectancy and substantial future care needs. Senior Judge Lush considered the evidence and commented that in cases such as this one, mutual dependency between P and her family members is inevitable and P's interests were invariably linked with those of her family members. Dismissing the deputy's application may have a negative impact on P – for instance, P's parents would have to resume work to maintain the family home and pay for P's brother's school fees; this would invariably result in an expensive care package being commissioned for P; and P would not benefit from her parents' time and care. The Judge therefore approved the application in this instance but also pressed upon the fact that this case should not be seen as a precedent for the payment of school fees or other expenses from P's injury award. What should be noted in this case is that the payment of the school fees and payments to maintain the family home were affordable and P's award of £5m remained intact.

78 David Ross v A [2015] EWCOP 46.

CHAPTER SEVEN

CHECKLIST FOR PRACTITIONERS: IS AN APPLICATION APPROPRIATE?

From her experience, the author sets out in this chapter a checklist of practical issues to address with a potential client in the early stages of a case. This list is not intended to be exhaustive and serves as a helpful guide when advising clients on whether a proposed gift might reasonably be approved by the Court of Protection.

7.1 – P's capacity to gift

First and foremost, discuss with your client if the proposed gift is straightforward and whether P has the capacity to authorise the gift themselves. Although obvious, this is a matter which can be easily overlooked in the first meeting as a result of an assumption made by your client.

As explained in Chapter 1.2, there is a presumption of capacity and P should be supported in making decisions by themselves. Even if P has been diagnosed with a medical condition or there is a registered Power of Attorney or a Deputyship Order in place, consider with your client whether P retains the capacity to make the decision in question, if sufficiently supported.

This was considered in the case of **Day v Royal College of Music [2013]**[79]. Although this is not a case brought before the Court of Protection and instead involved P's children challenging the validity of gifts made by P after P's death, it is relevant since it is a reminder to practitioners of the importance to discuss the different levels of capacity with clients from the outset.

In the case of **Day v Royal College of Music [2013]**, P had been making gifts to his attorney from a joint account held in the names of P and his attorney. The monies in that account belonged to P and P had gifted small amounts over a period of time to make use of tax exemptions. The total amount of gifts being challenged by P's children after his death was £36,000. It was the children's case that P lacked capacity when these gifts were made and the attorney had breached his fiduciary duty. After considering the evidence before him, the trial judge found that P had retained sufficient capacity to consent to the making of these gifts. This is because the gifts in question were relatively small, simple and straightforward.

> Author's note – Obtain further information from your client on the amount which they propose gifting. If P has the necessary capacity to consent to the gift, the attorney or deputy may neither need to make this decision on behalf of P nor make an application to the Court of Protection. P may require some support in making such decisions and the client should be advised to record key information including: (i) the conversations they had with P; (ii) what led them to conclude that P retains capacity; (iii) any tools or support which was provided to P to assist them with making the decision; and (iv) P's reasoning behind the decision. If in doubt regarding P's capacity, advise your client to seek a report on P's capacity to make the proposed gift.[80]

79 Day v Royal College of Music [2013] EWCA CIV 191.

80 See Chapter 2.3 and 2.4 for more information on how to procure such a report.

7.2 – Is there a restriction on gifting?

Ask to see a copy of the Power of Attorney instrument. Donors have the option to include specific preferences and/or restrictions in their Lasting of Power of Attorney. This is usually set out in section 7 of their Lasting of Power instrument. Prior to October 2007,[81] when Enduring Powers of Attorney could still be made, donors could include their restrictions or conditions in Part B of the Enduring Power of Attorney instrument.

Donors can record a "preference" in a Lasting Power of Attorney. However, their attorneys are not required to follow these recorded preferences but should keep them in mind, particularly when going through the best-interests checklist set out in section 4 of the Mental Capacity Act 2005. Donors can also record an "instruction" in their Lasting Power of Attorney. In contrast, attorneys are required to follow these instructions and not simply "keep them in mind". Instructions can be restrictive and should therefore be worded carefully. If the wording of an instruction restrains the attorney from carrying out their duty lawfully,[82] the Public Guardian may intervene and ask the Court of Protection to remove the "instructions" from the Lasting Power of Attorney before it is registered.

However, the position is different when it comes to placing *restrictions* on gifts made by an attorney (as opposed to extending an attorney's power to make a gift). In such circumstances, the Court is not likely to intervene and may yet allow the Lasting Power of Attorney to be registered. Once registered, these restrictions will reflect the donor's wishes and the attorney will be required to follow and respect them.

81 New Enduring Powers of Attorney can no longer be created. However, if a person had made an Enduring Power of Attorney before October 2007 (whether registered or not), it is still valid and can be used.

82 Caselaw shows that attempts made by donors to extend their attorney's statutory power to gift by including such instructions have failed.

Author's note – When making a best-interests decision for P, an attorney or deputy should consider the donor's past and present wishes and feelings which include any written statement made by them – such as statements made in the Lasting Power of Attorney or Enduring Power of Attorney. Should your client insist on a proposed gift which goes against the restrictions set out by the donor in their Power of Attorney, their application is not likely to succeed for several reasons including the Court's reluctance to depart from the wishes stated by someone at a time they had capacity. Deputyship Orders typically include standard authority on gifting.[83] Nonetheless, it is advisable to check the wording in the event that the Court of Protection made different provisions and placed specific restrictions in the Deputyship Order when the deputy was appointed.

7.3 – Is the proposed gift affordable?

If there are no restrictions placed in the Power of Attorney instrument or the Deputyship Order, take your client through the process of assessing whether the proposed gift is affordable. Ultimately, if the proposed gift is likely to have a negative financial impact on P, such an application is not likely to succeed. The author has already set out, in Chapter 6, the best-interests checklist to have regard to when making decisions on behalf of P. The factors specific to an application for the approval of a gift include: [84]

- The overall size of P's estate.
- P's medical condition and life expectancy.

83 See Chapter 3 for a deputy's statutory powers on gifting.

84 This is not exhaustive but it a helpful checklist.

- Whether P's medical condition is likely to improve or whether they suffer from a progressive illness.
- If P suffers from a progressive illness, what their future needs are likely to be.
- How it is anticipated that these future needs will be met.
- Whether any adaptations need to be made to P's current place of residence in anticipation of P's deterioration.
- Whether additional medical or recreational equipment will need to be purchased to improve P's quality of life now and in the future.
- An estimated costs of the above bearing in mind P's life expectancy.
- The likelihood that P may be required to move into a care or nursing home and its projected costs.
- Whether P is entitled to or receives CHC (NHS Continuing Healthcare) funding and if this is likely to be withdrawn.

Author's note – The Court of Protection will not be satisfied with basic and limited evidence, particularly where the proposed gift is substantial. The Court will expect to see evidence that the attorney or deputy has considered the full financial impact of the proposed gift on P's circumstances and whether an appropriate sum of money has been ring-fenced or will be made available to P to cover unforeseen expenses. This is why a thorough analysis of P's current and future needs as well as their corresponding costs should be carried out.

7.4 – P's Will and testamentary wishes

Consider the contents of P's Will with your client. If your client is an attorney or a deputy, they will be entitled to see a copy of P's Will.

Until as recently as 2017, an attorney did not have the automatic right to access P's Will unless P specifically gave this authority in their Lasting Power of Attorney. After all, a Will is a private and confidential document and should not be disclosed unless this has been agreed. However, it is recognised that P's testamentary wishes are a key factor for a decision-maker to consider when making financial decisions on behalf of P. Accordingly, in March 2017, [85] the SRA published an Ethics Guidance: "Access to and disclosure of an incapacitated person's will" for all authorised firms and their employees. The Guidance clarifies the circumstances in which a solicitor can disclose a copy of a client's Will to a property and affairs attorney or a deputy and acknowledges that a Will forms part of a donor's financial affairs. Unless the donor provides contrary instructions in their Power of Attorney instrument, the attorney is entitled to a copy of P's Will.

When considering an application to make a gift to someone else, it is important to discuss the contents of P's Will with your client. As stated by Senior Judge Lush in the case of **Re Joan Treadwell [2013]**[86], "*In the context of someone's property and affairs, I can think of no written statement that is more relevant or more important than a Will, and when testators make a Will, they have a reasonable expectation that their wishes will be respected.*[87]" P's Will was a factor of magnetic importance in this case.

The Court of Protection will be reluctant to deny P of their assets during their lifetime and depart from or intervene with P's testamentary wishes.

---

85 This Guidance was updated on 25 November 2019.

86 Re Joan Treadwell [2013] EWHC 2409.

87 Re Joan Treadwell [2013] EWHC 2409, para 88.

It is therefore important to discuss the following with your client to manage their expectations:

- Has the proposed gift in question been left to a specific beneficiary in P's Will? If so, the attorney or deputy should avoid frustrating P's testamentary wishes by gifting that specific gift to someone else.

- Is the proposed recipient of the gift a beneficiary of P's estate in the Will? If not, consider why P made that decision. It may be helpful to seek a copy of P's Will file (and their Letter of Wishes if one is in existence) which may set out P's reasoning or explanation as to why someone was excluded as a beneficiary. This would have been expressed by P at a time when they had capacity and should be respected by the client.

- Explain that the role of the Court of Protection is not to "correct" matters. There may be instances where a gift is being proposed because the proposed recipient was left out of the Will and the applicant wishes to rectify the situation. It is important to remind the client that the Court of Protection's role is make decisions which are in P's best interests and not to "correct" P's testamentary wishes.

Author's note – P's Will is a key document and applicants are expected to attach a copy to their application.[88] Although attorneys and deputies are entitled to see a copy of the Will, they may not know if there is one in existence. Clients should be advised to take active steps in locating a Will to demonstrate that measures have been taken to consider P's testamentary wishes. This can be done by conducting a thorough search of P's papers, speaking to P's family, friends, and the family solicitor. A will search with the National Will Register is a helpful tool which should also be considered. The National Will Register have over 10 million wills registered in their system and provide a specialist Court of Protection service to support attorneys/deputies in searching for a Will.[89]

7.5 – Funding the application

Discuss with your client whether the proposed gift justifies the associated costs involved in making an application to the Court of Protection. The costs rules in Court of Protection applications are different to the costs rules in civil litigation. The general rule which applies to applications involving P's property and affairs (and therefore the approval of a gift) is:

> *"Where proceedings concern P's property and affairs the general rule is that the costs of the proceedings, or that part of the proceedings what*

88 This is usually attached to form COP1 A and form COP1 C. See Chapter 8 for further information on these forms.

89 The National Will Register and Certainty Will Search can be used by the public and professionals to register Wills and search Wills in the UK. A search can be carried out through their website: https://www.nationalwillregister.co.uk/search-for-a-will/

concerns P's property and affairs, shall be paid by P or charged to P's estate."[90]

From the outset, practitioners should raise the following main points with a client:

- Legal costs incurred by a party in applications of this nature can run into tens of thousands of pounds, particularly if contested by other parties. Since P's estate is likely to bear the costs of the application (which extend not only to the client's costs but also the costs of the other parties involved in the proceedings as well as the Official Solicitors' costs if they are appointed to represent P), do these costs justify the amount of the proposed gift? This is a balancing exercise to carry out with your client. You should make your client aware that by making the application, P's estate is being reduced not only by the amount of the proposed gift but also by the legal costs which will be charged to it.

- The general rule on costs may give a client the illusion that they will not be responsible for costs since these will be borne by P's estate. It is important to remind clients that under rule 19.5 of the Court of Protection Rules 2017, the Court may depart from the general rule depending on the circumstances of the case and make a costs order that your client should bear their own costs.[91] Is this a risk the client is willing to take?

90 Rule 19.2 of the Court of Protection Rules 2017

91 See rule 19.5 (2) for further information on the "conduct of the parties". The author addresses this in detail in Chapter 10.2.

Author's note – Before issuing proceedings, it is prudent to seek the views of those your client will be required to notify on the proposed gift. If they are likely to object, discuss the financial implications and risks with your client to enable them to take a commercial view and make an informed decision on whether they wish to proceed with the application.

7.6 – Potential conflict and hostility within the family

Parties engaged in litigation will undoubtedly find themselves involved in court proceedings which may take several months to conclude. Whilst their legal team will be available to advise, assist and represent them in the court proceedings, clients should also be prepared for the friction and hostility they may face from P's close family members and friends.

As part of the application process, the applicant will be required to notify key people of their proposal make a gift using P's funds.[92] Depending on what is being sought in the application, the persons to be notified are likely to be P's close family members. The following list of people is ordered according to the presumed closeness in terms of their relationship to P. They should be notified in descending order (as appropriate to P's circumstances)[93] –

(a) spouse or civil partner;

(b) person who is not a spouse or a civil partner but who has been living with P as if they were;

(c) parent or guardian;

92 Court of Protection Rules 2017, rule 9.10 and Practice Direction 9B.

93 Court of Protection Rules 2017, Practice Direction 9B, para 7.

(d) child;

(e) brother or sister;

(f) grandparent or grandchild;

(g) aunt or uncle;

(h) niece or nephew;

(i) step-parent; and

(j) half-brother or half-sister.[94]

In addition, other persons may need to be notified – for instance, someone who provides P with care; P's attorney or deputy (if the application is being made by someone else); or a beneficiary of P's Will who is likely to be affected by the proposed gift.

Given that the application is about reducing P's assets, it comes as no surprise that such an application may not always be well received and are likely to be objected to. When submitting an objection, the respondents will be required to file and serve evidence. The author has seen witness statements which often dig up past issues or family arguments which a client may find upsetting. It is therefore good practice for practitioners to go beyond advising a client on their legal position and brace them for the potential conflict and hostility which they may encounter in an application.

94 Guidance Notes on completing form COP1 Application Form, page 10.

7.7 – Is permission required?

After considering the above issues with your client, if their instructions are to make an application, as a final check, consider if your client will be required to seek the Court of Protection's permission to make the application in question.[95] Under rule 8.2(b)(i) of the Court of Protection Rules 2017, applications involving P's property and affairs (such as an application to make a gift) will not require the Court of Protection's permission. Moreover, in the author's experience, applications for the making of gifts are generally made by an attorney or a deputy and these applicants are exempt from requiring the permission of the Court of Protection. Seeking permission will therefore not be an issue in cases of this nature[96] and the next stage will be to prepare the application – which is what the next chapter of this book addresses.

95 Refer to section 50 of the Mental Capacity Act 2005 and the Court of Protection Rules 2017 as well as their corresponding Practice Directions.

96 Careful consideration should be given if the application includes health and welfare issues. The author does not address the procedure for seeking permission in this book since the subject matter involves P's property and affairs. However, readers are referred to the Court of Protection Rules 2017, Part 8 for further information on applying for permission to start proceedings should this be relevant to their application.

CHAPTER EIGHT

PREPARING THE APPLICATION

This chapter addresses the forms which an applicant is required to complete and the evidence to be collated by them to support their application. Practitioners should familiarise themselves with Part 9 of the Court of Protection Rules 2017 and Practice Directions 9E which set out the procedure to follow when starting proceedings in the Court of Protection.

8.1 – Pre-action communications

Before the application is drafted, as mentioned in Chapter 7.5, it may be helpful to approach the parties to a proposed application to gauge their initial reaction. This is a useful exercise to undertake, particularly if your client has indicated that the potential respondents are likely to object to the application. From experience, there is merit in making initial contact with the other parties, if only to:

- "Soften" the blow for when your client's application is subsequently served on them.
- Establish whether they would be willing to consider some other proposal which would result in an agreed application being submitted. Although submitting an agreed application does not guarantee that the Court of Protection will approve the gift,[97] it goes a long way to showing to the Court of Protection that those

97 See the case of PBC v JMA and others [2018] EWCOP 19. Even though there was an agreement in place, the Court listed the matter for an attending hearing before making a decision.

closely involved in P's life have been consulted and are in agreement. This is likely to add some weight to your client's application.

- Assist with preparing the application given that your client will have been made aware of the objections which the other parties are likely to raise and these can be addressed in their evidence, if appropriate.

- You will have the opportunity to re-assess the prospects of your client succeeding with their application and discuss whether it is financially viable to pursue the application.

8.2 – Forms to be completed

The author lists below the forms which an applicant or their legal representative will be required to complete to start an application. The forms are straightforward and their purpose is to set out key and relevant information which will assist the Court with making a best-interests decision.

These forms are:

- Form COP1 (Application Form).

- Form COP1A (Supporting information for property and financial affairs applications).

- Form COP1C (Supporting information for statutory will, codicil, gifts, deed of variation or settlement of property).

- Form COP3 (Assessment of capacity).

- Form COP24 (Witness Statement).

In the next sections, the author will provide guidance on what to include in the relevant forms and the common pitfalls to watch out for when completing the forms.

8.3 – Form COP1

Form COP1 is the start to the proceedings. This is a key document and careful consideration must be given to the various sections within the form when completing it. In particular, in section 4, the applicant should state clearly and concisely, what (a) order or declaration they are seeking from the Court of Protection; and (b) how such an order will benefit P. Be specific about what you are seeking and avoid seeking broad powers or orders from the Court of Protection.

You are only required to summarise the key and pertinent points in section 4 of the form and it is important to make sure that it is drafted in a balanced manner. The applicant will have the opportunity to set out their position in detail in form COP24 (their witness statement).

Another key section in this form which will require careful consideration is section 5. The author has already set out the potential respondents and people to be notified.[98] In cases of this nature, applicants should also refer to Practice Direction 9E of the Court of Protection Rules 2017 and name the beneficiaries of P's estate who are likely to be materially or adversely affected.[99] It is important to make sure that the relevant people are listed at tables 5.2A and 5.2B. Failure to include some of them (or failure to explain why they have not been included) is likely to result in delays and the applicant incurring substantial costs after the application is issued.

98 See Chapter 7.6, Practice Direction 9B of the Court of Protection Rules 2017 and the Guidance Notes on completing form COP1 Application Form, page 9-10.

99 Practice Direction 9E of the Court of Protection Rule 2017, para 9(a) – (c).

Key points for applicants to note in respect of section 5:

- If P's child or sibling is to be notified, you should ensure that all the children or siblings in that category are notified unless there is good reason not to do so.

- Do not limit notification to only family members based on their presumed closeness to P. In some instances, P may be closer to friends than family members and consider notifying them of the application.

- If an applicant chooses not to notify someone based on their presumed closeness to P,[100] a valid explanation should be provided in their witness evidence.

- The applicant should seek to identify at least three persons who are likely to have an interest in being notified that an application has been issued.

- A person who has been named as a respondent in table 5.2A should not also be listed as a person to be notified in table 5.2B.

> Author's note – If the applicant is seeking an order for their costs to be charged to P's estate pursuant to rule 19.2 of the Court of Protection Rules 2017, ensure this is included and made clear in section 4 of form COP1.

100 Practice Direction 9B, paragraph 7.

8.4 – Form COP1A

The purpose of this form is to furnish the Court with information on P's financial circumstances given that the order being sought will inadvertently affect P financially.

From experience, the attorney or deputy is better placed to complete form COP1A (in particular sections 4 and 5) since they will have up to date information on P's financial status and are also likely to be aware of who are involved in P's wellbeing and visit P.

> Author's note – If an applicant does not have sufficient information on P's finances but is aware of the person or organisation who holds this information, consider making an interim application seeking an order authorising the applicant to seek such information from that particular person or organisation before the application can progress. There is the option to seek an urgent interim order in section 1.3 of form COP1.

8.5 – Form COP1C

This form serves as a checklist to ensure that relevant documents and information are submitted to support the application.[101] The Court of Protection will pay careful attention to them and it is essential they are included to ensure that the application is dealt with in a timely and efficient manner. If certain documents cannot be put before the Court of Protection because they cannot be located or are simply not in existence, make sure that this is addressed in the applicant's witness statement. As mentioned above, there is also the option to seek an interim order for the

101 See section 4 of form COP1C and Practice Direction 9E of the Court of Protection Rules 2017.

disclosure of certain documents to either the applicant or to the Court of Protection.[102]

8.6 – Form COP3

This is a vital part of the application. As mentioned in Chapter 1.2, there is a presumption of capacity and the Court of Protection will only have jurisdiction if P lacks capacity. It is therefore important to put before the Court of Protection evidence that P lacks the capacity to make the proposed gift in the present circumstances.

A completed form COP3[103] will confirm whether, on the balance of probabilities, P lacks the required capacity to make the proposed gift. The applicant should make sure that the appropriate expert is instructed[104] and from experience, if the proposed gift is of substantial value, consider instructing the consultant under whose care P is.

Before form COP3 is sent to the assessor for their completion,[105] the applicant will be required to complete sections 1-3 (Part A). The author has already highlighted, in Chapter 2.4, key information which will assist the assessor with reporting on P's capacity to make a decision on gifting. Although such information will be included in section 3 of form COP3, the author finds that preparing a separate and detailed letter of instructions and setting out the legal test to be applied[106] goes a long way towards obtaining a robust report, particularly if the application is likely be disputed.

102 See the author's note in Chapter 8.3.

103 Form COP3 was updated in July 2023.

104 See Chapter 2.3 for who can assess capacity.

105 The assessor will be expected to complete Part B of the form.

106 See Chapter 2.2 for the legal test to apply.

Upon receipt of the completed form COP3 from the assessor, check that detailed information is included in section 6 and ensure the report deals specifically with:

- The decisions which P cannot make.
- Whether P can understand the relevant information for the decision which needs to be made.
- Whether P can retain the relevant information for the decision which needs to be made.
- Whether P can use and weigh the relevant information for the decision which needs to be made.
- Whether P can communicate the decision which needs to be made (whether verbally, using sign language or by any other means).
- The support which the assessor gave to P to help them understand the relevant information.
- Other steps which the assessor considers should be taken to support P in making the decision.
- Whether an impairment of or disturbance in the functioning of the mind or brain is stopping P from making the decision.
- Whether P expressed any relevant views.
- Whether P is likely to regain capacity in the future.
- When and how P was assessed.

8.7 – Form COP24

This form gives the applicant the opportunity to provide the Court of Protection with background information on P and explain why making the proposed gift is in P's best interests. Before preparing their evidence, the applicant should ensure that they have gone through the decision-making process and address in their statement the relevant factors which the Court of Protection will have regard to for this particular application.[107]

It is important to put forward evidence which is relevant to the application in question. There may be a temptation for an applicant to vent their frustration in respect of past family disputes which are not related to the application. Applicants should be advised that the Court of Protection will primarily be concerned with P's circumstances and how the application will be in P's best interests. The Court of Protection's jurisdiction does not extend to resolving family disputes and "making right" a wrong which P is perceived to have done in the past.

The author has already listed a few factors which an applicant should have regard to before making an application[108] and sets out below key evidence which should be collated and put before the Judge to support their application: [109]

Family relationships

- A family tree to assist the Court with understanding P's family dynamics.

---

107 See Chapter 6.

108 See Chapters 7.3 and 7.4.

109 This is not intended to be an exhaustive list. The evidence to be collated will depend on the order being sought and the facts of the case.

- Explain the relationship between P and the proposed recipient. The Court will be reluctant to reduce P's capital in favour of relatively remote relations.

- If the proposed recipient has a compelling need, provide relevant supporting evidence.

- Set out any direct evidence from P in respect of gifting to the proposed recipient – this can be in the form of a written record from P such as a preference in their Power of Attorney, a letter addressed to a family member or a friend expressing this wish.

- Set out what P was in the habit of doing, particularly if the proposal reflects historical gifting to the proposed recipient.

P's current needs:

- A report on P's current medical condition, their care plan and how their needs are being met.

- If P is in a care home, explain how this is being funded – for instance, from P's income or capital.

- Set out any additional expenses which P is funding and whether they are currently affordable.

P's life expectancy and future needs:

- A social and care assessment report on P's predicted life expectancy,[110] their predicted future medical, social and recreational needs.

110 In the case of Re JDS [2012] COPLR 383, the Court dismissed an application to gift the sum of £325,000 to P's parents on the basis that P

- Set out how much these future needs are likely cost and whether P will be able to afford them.

- If P is in a privately funded care home, given that inflation of care home fees is a real issue, explain how the likely level of increases in care fees will be met by P.

- If P is currently receiving CHC funding, provide information on whether P is likely to be discharged to local authority accommodation or other fee-paying accommodation and how much P will then be expected to pay to fund his care in the future.

P's finances:

- A schedule showing P's estimated net yearly income, outgoings and capital.

- Set out what % the proposed gift represents in comparison with P's total assets – the Court will be reluctant to deprive P of a substantial part of their estate.

- A financial report to show that even after the proposed gift is made, P will be left with sufficient funds to cover his current needs as well as the identified future needs – preferably in the form of a "before and after" schedule after factoring in tax implications.

- Evidence that there will be additional funds remaining as a "cushion" to cover unforeseen expenses during P's lifetime.

---

was only 20 at the time of the application and he was expected to live for another 25-30 years.

P's testamentary wishes and tax implications

- If P has made a Will, put forward evidence that the proposed gift will not affect or frustrate P's testamentary wishes.

- Seek professional advice, if appropriate, and confirm whether there will be any tax implications as a result of the proposed gift.

The above relevant information should be set out in the form of a witness statement with documents attached as exhibits. Practitioners who have completed form COP24 in the past will be aware of its restrictive format which can make a long statement difficult to read and follow. In the author's experience, preparing a separate witness statement sworn by a statement of truth and attaching it to a completed form COP24 is usually accepted by the Court of Protection.

8.8 – Other evidence which the Court of Protection may have regard to

Depending on the value of the proposed gift and the nature of P's estate, it may be appropriate to put forward evidence from someone other than the applicant. From experience, evidence from neutral parties who do not have an interest in the outcome of the application or evidence from professionals can prove to be helpful.

There may be value in obtaining evidence from people closely connected to P. For instance P may have, at a time when they had capacity, expressed their wishes or feelings whilst conversing with a close family friend, their carer, their social worker or other professionals (such as a family solicitor, an accountant or a financial advisor). A witness statement from them or a copy of their care/medical notes recording these conversations may prove to be helpful and consider exhibiting them to the applicant's witness statement.

8.9 – Short applications

Attorneys or deputies who wish to make a gift which falls outside the scope of their powers (or which does not fall within the de minimis principle)[111] will require the Court of Protection's approval. As seen from above, this involves a formal application which can be time consuming and costly given the various forms which need to be completed.

There is a marked difference between a proposed gift which involves a large part of P's assets and a proposed gift which is not substantial and is easily affordable – but does it fall within the de minimis principle. This raises the question whether the effort and expense of a formal application is justifiable in such circumstances.

The law recognises that making a formal application for routine and simple gifts may not be in P's best interests, particularly given the costs implications.[112] Very often, these gifts are being contemplated by P's attorneys or deputies who are fully aware of P's family dynamics and financial circumstances. They will also have discussed the matter with those close to P and considered whether the proposed gift is reasonable, affordable and not likely to be disputed.

Practice Direction 9D of the Court of Protection Rules 2017 provides a short and simplified procedure for deputies and attorneys to follow when gifts of this nature are being considered. Such gifts are described as:

> *"applications to make a gift or loan from P's assets, provided that the sum in question is not disproportionately large when compared to the size of P's estate as a whole"*[113]

---

111 See Chapter 5.3 for further information on the de minimis principle.

112 The author addresses the implications of legal costs in Court of Protection proceedings in Chapter 10

113 Practice Direction 9D, para 4(g) – this applies to deputies.

or

> *"applications to make a gift from P's assets, provided that the sum in question is not disproportionately large when compared to the size of P's estate as a whole"*[114]

The main points to be aware of when making an application under Practice 9D are:

- There is an issue fee payable when the application is made.[115]
- The applicant is still required to complete and submit form COP1 together with supporting evidence.
- Such supporting evidence should include up to date information on P's assets, their financial circumstances and whether any major decisions involving P has been or is likely to be made and what their implications are or will be on P's finances – consider whether form COP1A or a short witness statement will be more cost effective.
- The applicant is not required to complete forms COP1A, COP1C or COP3.
- The applicant is also not required to serve the application form on anyone or notify anyone that the application has been made.
- Instead, the Court will make a decision, after reviewing the application, as to whether someone ought to be notified and given

114 Practice Direction 9D, para 5(b) – this applies to attorneys. Note the slight difference in respect of the making of a loan by deputies.

115 Information stands correct as of November 2023. Fees were updated from 30 September 2021 and it is advisable to check COP44 for the applicable fee before issuing your application.

the opportunity to respond. In such a case, the Court will give further directions.

- Otherwise, if the Court is satisfied that the proposed gift is in P's best interests, an order authorising the gift will be made on paper.

For further information on the procedure for short applications, readers are referred to paragraph 8 of Practice Direction 9D of the Court of Protection Rules 2017.

CHAPTER NINE

ISSUING PROCEEDINGS AND GETTING TO THE FINAL STAGE

9.1 – Issuing and the application fee

Once the forms are completed and the application is ready, submit a hard copy by post to the central office of the Court of Protection in London.[116] Their details are as follows:

Address – Court of Protection, PO Box 70185, First Avenue House, 42-49 High Holborn, London, WC1A 9JA.

Email – courtofprotectionenquiries@justice.gov.uk

Enquiries – 0300 456 4600

There is a court application fee in the sum of £371[117] payable at the time the papers are submitted. On receipt of the papers, the Court of Protection will issue the application and allocate a case number to it – this is normally stamped on the first page of form COP1. This is when the proceedings formally begin.

116 Deputyship applications can be submitted online but it is still a requirement to submit a hard copy of an application which relates to property and affairs matters.

117 Information stands correct as of November 2023. Fees were updated from 30 September 2021 and it is advisable to check COP44 for the applicable fee before issuing your application.

The Court of Protection will return a copy of the issued application together with initial case management directions. Such directions usually include (but are not limited to):

- Whether P should be joined as a party to the proceedings. In applications of this nature, P will almost always be added as a party. If there is no one suitable to represent P, the Court of Protection will invite the Official Solicitor to represent P in the proceedings.[118]

- Serving a copy on the application on the respondents listed in form COP1.

- Notifying P as well as those listed in section 5.2B in form COP1.

9.2 – Service and Notification

It should not be assumed that the Court of Protection will serve a copy of the application on the relevant parties once it is issued. The Court will serve documents during the course of the proceedings but only in limited circumstances – such as serving an order or a judgment, an acknowledgment of service or a notice of hearing.

It is the responsibility of the applicant to serve a copy of the application on anyone named as a respondent in section 5.2A of form COP1 and notify those listed in section 5.2B of the proceedings. The Court will set a timeframe for the applicant to comply with service and notification, failing which Part 9 of the Court of Protection Rules will follow.

118 Note: The Official can decline to act as P's litigation friend if there is not security for their costs or in cases where the value of P's estate is not substantial enough to justify the Official Solicitor's costs.

Serving papers on a respondent:

As a reminder, respondents are those who have an interest in the application or who are likely to be affected by the outcome of the proceedings. They will have the opportunity to be joined as a party if they wish to participate in the proceedings. Unless the Court of Protection sets other directions, it is the applicant's responsibility to serve the application on the respondents "*as soon as practicable and in any event within 14 days of the date on which the application form was issued.*"[119]

Key points to be aware of:

- The applicant should serve a copy of the full application which will include all the forms as well as the witness statement(s) and exhibits.
- In addition, the respondent should be sent form COP5 (Acknowledgment of Service/notification) for their completion together with the Guidance notes on completing form COP5.[120]
- The applicant should then complete a certificate of service (form COP20B)[121] and file it with the Court of Protection within 7 days beginning with the date on which the application was served.[122]

---

119 Court of Protection Rules 2017, Part 9, para 9.6(1)

120 These can be found on the gov.uk website.

Section 2.2 of form COP20B should be completed.

122 Court of Protection Rules 2017, Part 9, para 9.6(2)

Notifying other persons of the application:

The applicant will be required to notify those listed in section 5.2B of form COP1 "*as soon as practicable and in any event within 14 days of the date on which the application form was issued.*"[123]

Key points to be aware of:

- An applicant is not required to serve a full copy of the application on those to be notified.
- Instead, the applicant should complete form COP15. This is a notice informing the recipient that an application involving P has been issued by the Court of Protection.
- Make sure to include the following information in the form: (i) the application involves P's property and affairs and (ii) what order(s) are being sought.[124]
- In addition to form COP15, send a copy of form COP 5 together with the Guidance notes on completing form COP5.
- The applicant should then complete a certificate of service (form COP20B)[125] and file it with the Court within 7 days beginning with the date on which notification was given.[126]

Notifying P

If the Court has directed that P is to be joined as a party to the proceedings (from experience, this is what is normally directed in applications for

123 Court of Protection Rules 2017, Part 9, para 9.10 (1).

124 Court of Protection Rules 2017, Part 9, para 9.10(1)(b)(c).

125 Section 2.3 of form COP20B should be completed.

126 Court of Protection Rules 2017, Part 9, para 9.10 (3).

the approval of substantial gifts) and the Official Solicitor has been invited (and agrees) to represent P in the proceedings, the applicant will be expected to serve a copy of the full application on the Official Solicitor[127] and directions to this effect will be made by the Court of Protection once the application is issued. The applicant will not be required to notify P in this instance.

In the absence of such specific directions, the applicant will be expected to notify P that an application involving him has been issued by the Court of Protection and applicants should be aware of the following key points:

- They are required to notify P in person and explain matters using means most appropriate to P's circumstances. If the applicant is not able to effect personal service, an agent should be instructed to notify P in their place.

- A full copy of the application need not be served on P. Instead, the applicant will be required complete form COP14 which should include the following information: (i) the application involves P's property and affairs; (ii) what order(s) are being sought; and (iii) how P will be affected if the application is approved by the Court of Protection.[128]

- As mentioned above, form COP14 cannot simply be posted to P. It should be presented to P in person together with a copy of form COP 5 and the Guidance notes on completing form COP5.

127 Readers are referred to paras 17-21 of the "Appointment of the Official Solicitor in property and affairs proceedings:practice note" for further information on how to serve a copy of the relevant papers on the Official Solicitor.

128 Court of Protection Rules 2017, Part 9, para 9.10(1)(b)(c).

- The applicant (or the person effecting service) should then complete a certificate of service (form COP20A) and file it with the Court within 7 days beginning with the date on which P was notified.[129] Form COP20A is more detailed than form COP20B and careful consideration should be given when completing it.

9.3 – Responding to the application

Those who are served or notified of proceedings will be expected to complete and file form COP5 to inform the Court of their views on the application. This must be done no more than 14 days after the application was served on them or notification of the application was given to them.[130] If they do not respond, they will not have a say in the court proceedings and will be bound by any decision made by the Court of Protection.

The respondent or the person notified will normally provide the following information in the form:

- Whether they consent to the application.

- Whether they oppose the application or seek a different order. In such circumstances, they will be to required to file a witness statement with evidence on which they intend to rely within 28 days of being served with the application.[131]

- Indicate whether they wish to be joined as a party to the proceedings.

---

129 Court of Protection Rules 2017, Part 7, para 7.10.

130 Court of Protection Rules 2017, Part 9, para 9.12(2).

131 Court of Protection Rules 2017, Part 9, para 9.12(5).

A completed form COP5 will assist the Court of Protection with determining if the case is to proceed to a hearing and if so, how to manage the case in the future.

9.4 – Case management directions and hearings

Upon receipt of the completed forms COP5, the Court of Protection will serve a copy on the applicant and the other parties to the proceedings. If a party objects to the application, seeks a different order or the Court of Protection forms the view that the matter should be listed for an attended hearing, the Court of Protection is likely to allocate the case to the Property and Affairs Pathway and set further directions as to the management of the case, which will typically include:

- Adding someone who has applied to be made a party to the current court proceedings.
- Listing the matter for a Dispute Resolution Hearing to determine whether the case can be resolved and to try and avoid unnecessary litigation.[132]
- Directing that the case is transferred to the most appropriate regional court depending on where the parties are based.[133]

132 The Court of Protection will usually wait for a period of at least 3 months before listing the matter for a Dispute Resolution Hearing to allow the parties time to engage with one another and potentially narrow down the issues in dispute.

133 Regional hubs are located at Leeds Combined Court Centre, Newcastle Combined Court Centre, Manchester Civil Justice Centre, Reading County and Family Court, Bristol Civil & Family Justice Centre, Cardiff Civil & Family Justice Centre, Birmingham Civil and Family Justice Centre.

- Filing of further evidence which each party wishes to rely upon.
- Disclosure to take place, if appropriate.
- Listing the matter for a hearing for the determination of certain preliminary issues, if appropriate.
- Thereafter, listing the matter for a directions and/or a final hearing.

It is not unusual in contested applications for there to be more than one hearing before a final decision is made. Hearings typically take place to assist the Court and the parties to identify and focus on the central issues in the case; set a timetable to a final hearing; for the Court to make interim orders or declarations to ensure that P's interests are secured (if appropriate); and deal with any interim application made by one of the parties whilst the proceedings are ongoing.

If counsel was not involved in the preparation of the application, now might be a good time to instruct counsel to represent the applicant or a party to the proceedings in court hearings. Readers are referred to the Court of Protection Rules 2017 for further information on how to prepare for a hearing and, in particular, how to prepare the hearing bundle and the preliminary documents.[134]

134 Court of Protection Rules 2017, Practice Direction 4B.

9.5 – Alternative Dispute Resolution ("ADR")

The Court does not have the power to impose ADR on the parties. However, it is advisable for parties to engage in ADR to attempt to reach an early agreement. It is not unusual for the Court of Protection to initially list the matter for a dispute resolution hearing or direct the parties to attend a round table meeting or an advocates meeting.

Communications between parties to avoid unnecessary litigation are very much encouraged by the Court. To narrow down the issues prior to a hearing, Judges are known to routinely include in a court order a standard direction requiring the parties to attend Court an hour before a hearing to engage in discussions.

It is important to advise an applicant or a party to the proceedings of the importance of engaging in alternative dispute resolution and coming to a compromise. Parties may experience a false sense of security thinking that their costs will ultimately be borne by P's estate. However, this is not the case as the general rules on costs are not as black and white as one might think.[135] Parties should consider how the dispute can be resolved in a speedy and proportionate manner. In doing so, they should put aside their personal grievances against one another; focus on the facts before them and consider whether the proposed gift or a gift of a smaller value is in P's best interests given P's past behaviour and relationship with the proposed recipient.

---

135 The author addresses the costs risks in Chapter 11.

> Author's note – An agreement reached by all the parties does not necessarily mean that the Court of Protection will approve the gift without a hearing. Ultimately, this is a decision for the Court of Protection to make, having regard to the factors listed in section 4 of the Mental Capacity Act 2005. From experience, the Official Solicitor who is representing P in the proceedings will take the lead in preparing a comprehensive report to the Court of Protection addressing the factors which have been applied to P's individual case and setting out the reasoning behind why approving the gift will be in P's best interests. Such a comprehensive report is likely to be accepted by the Court of Protection but as caselaw has shown, the Court may still list the matter for an attended hearing to hear further evidence.[136]

9.6 – Final hearing

If an agreement is not reached and approved by the Court of Protection, the matter will proceed to a final hearing. A hearing fee in the sum of £494[137] will be payable by the applicant. Depending on the value of the gift, the volume of disclosed evidence and the number of witnesses expected to give oral evidence, a final hearing may be listed for several days. The judgment may be given at a later date should the Judge require further time to consider matters.

As a reminder, the Court of Protection will approve the proposed gift if it is in P's best interests to do so. However, it should be noted that applications of this nature are not an "*all or nothing*" case. A range of final orders can be made in applications of this nature and Judges are known to be creative when it comes to finding a solution which will preserve P's interests whilst also taking into account the circumstances of a proposed recipient who has a compelling need for some financial assistance.

136 See the case of PBC v JMA and others [2018] EWCOP 19.

137 Information stands correct as of November 2023.

An example is the case of **Re AK [2014]**[138]. This case involved P, a 11-year old boy,[139] whose parents are of Pakistani origin. P had been awarded a lump sum of just over £1m as clinical damages. In addition, he received periodical payments from the NHS Trust which would continue for the rest of his life (this was calculated on the basis that P was not likely to live beyond the age of 15).

An application was made by P's professional deputy seeking the Court's approval to gift the sum of £150,000 to P's parents which would be used by P's parents to purchase a plot of land in Pakistan and build a suitably adapted property for P to have use of whenever he would visit Pakistan. It was envisaged that P and his parents would spend several months a year in Pakistan and it was submitted that building a property in Pakistan to cater to P's specific needs would be in his best interests. The intention was for P's parents to own the property in their name since P was a minor.

This application was contested by the Official Solicitor appointed to represent P on the basis that making an outright gift to P's parents would in effect deny P of his capital during his lifetime and there was no guarantee that the monies would be used by P's parents to procure a property for P's use and enjoyment.

Senior Judge Lush heard the arguments in favour of and against the proposed gift. He came to the conclusion that having a suitably adapted property in Pakistan for P's use would benefit P. However, it was recognised that P would be denied of his capital during his lifetime and the ultimate beneficiary of the property would be his parents. Senior Judge Lush therefore came up with a solution – he approved the application but on the basis that instead of an outright gift, the deputy could advance an interest free loan in the sum of £150,000 to P's parents to purchase

138 Re AK [2014] EWHC B11 (COP).

139 Although the Mental capacity Act 2005 applies only to persons aged 16 and over, the Court can still appoint a deputy if the child/P is unlikely to manage their financial affairs when they reach adulthood.

the plot of land and build a property in their name. In return, the parents would repay the loan over a period of 10 years (£15,000 a year). Since the parents could not afford the repayment, Senior Judge Lush went further and approved annual gifts in the sum of £15,000 to the parents from P's surplus income. By putting this financial arrangement in place, the Judge ensured that P retained his capital and it was a way to ensure that P's parents would use the funds for their intended purpose.

> Author's note – A lesson to be learnt from the above is that throughout the proceedings, it is important to keep an open mind as to how a settlement can be reached without the need for unnecessary litigation. The above is a classic example of how parties should be creative when engaging in ADR.

CHAPTER TEN

COSTS IN COURT OF PROTECTION PROCEEDINGS

Litigation can be costly and it is important for a party to be aware of how a Judge is likely to deal with the issue of costs at the conclusion of a case, whether they are successful or not.

Many will be familiar with the phrase "*costs follow the event*" or "*the loser pays the winner's costs*" in general litigation. However, in the Court of Protection, different costs rules apply depending on the nature of the application: whether the application involves (i) P's property and affairs; or (ii) P's health and welfare. Each of these has a different costs implication which is set out in rule 19 of the Court of Protection Rules 2017. Since this book is on the making of gifts which involves P's finances, the author will focus on the costs rules relating to property and affairs. However, readers are referred to Part 19.3 and 19.4 of the Court of Protection Costs Rules 2017 for further information on the costs rules relating to health and welfare applications.[140]

This chapter will address (i) the general rules on costs in property and affairs; (ii) when the Court of Protection may depart from the general rule on costs, therefore placing a party at risk of a costs order against them; (iii) cases where the Court of Protection has departed from the general rule on costs; and (iv) what a party is likely to recover from P's estate.

140 The general rule states that each party bears their own costs in proceedings involving P's personal welfare unless there are good reasons to depart from this.

10.1 – Property and affairs applications

The starting point is:

> "*Where proceedings concern P's property and affairs the general rule states that the costs of the proceedings, or that part of the proceedings that concerns P's property and affairs, shall be paid by P or charged to P's estate.*"[141]

In brief, any party who issues an application or defends it can seek an order that their costs are paid by P's estate. The costs mentioned in the above rule extend not only to the applicant's costs but also to the costs of the other parties to the proceedings as well as the costs of the Official Solicitor or P's litigation friend if P is joined as a party to the proceedings. Legal costs (particularly in contested applications) can run into tens of thousands of pounds and the total costs can amount to a staggering sum which P's estate will be expected to bear. It is therefore of utmost importance that careful consideration is given as to whether pursuing an application or contesting an application is proportionate and/or is in P's best interests.

An applicant or the parties to the court proceedings may form the view that since they will not be responsible for the payment of their costs – whether they win or lose – there is no financial loss in fighting the case to a final hearing. This false illusion is recognised by the law and to deter parties from engaging in court proceedings without due care, the rules on costs in the Court of Protection go further and provide for instances when the Court of Protection may depart from the general rule.

141 Court of Protection Rules 2017, Part 19, para 19.2.

10.2 – Departing from the general rule

Costs in Court of Protection proceedings remain at the discretion of the Judge and the Court has full power to depart from the general rule and determine by whom and to what extent the costs are to be paid.[142] Although the Court of Protection does not make a habit of departing from the general rule (after all, the risk of an adverse costs order should not deter a party from bringing a dispute to the Court of Protection and to uphold what they feel is in P's best interests), there are instances when the Court will not hesitate to apply their discretion. In doing so, the Court will have regard to the following:

a. The conduct of the parties;

b. Whether a party has succeeded on part of their case, even if not wholly successful; and

c. The role of any public body involved in the proceedings.[143]

The Court of Protection Rules 2017 go further and describe the conduct of the parties as being:

- Conduct before, as well as during, proceedings;
- Whether it was reasonable for a party to raise, pursue or contest a particular matter;
- The manner in which the party has made or responded to an application or a particular issue;

142 Mental Capacity Act 2005, section 55.

143 Court of Protection Rules 2017, Part 19.5(1)

- Whether a party who has succeeded in their application or response to an application, in whole or in part, exaggerated any matter contained in the application or response; and

- Any failure by a party to comply with a rule, practice direction or court order.[144]

With litigation becoming more and more expensive, the author has noted that the Court of Protection will, in some cases, take the lead and place parties on notice of costs from the very outset of a case by including the following paragraph in initial court directions:

> "*The parties are reminded that whilst the usual order for costs in property and affairs cases is that the parties' costs shall be paid by [P]'s funds, the court can depart from that position where, for example, a party has unreasonably pursued or contested a particular issue.*"

The conduct of the parties (before and during proceedings) is therefore a key factor which the Court of Protection will consider when making a costs order at the conclusion of a matter, particularly where one of the parties asks the Judge to depart from the general rule. Parties who are legally represented will be advised on how to conduct court proceedings in a reasonable manner and are not likely to be penalised if the issues they raise are pertinent to P's circumstances.

144 Court of Protection Rules 2017, Part 19.5(2)(a)-(e).

Author's note – Departing from the general rule is not limited to an order that a party (such as the applicant or the objector) is not allowed to recover their costs from P's estate resulting in them bearing their own costs. The costs order can extend to the party paying not only their own costs but the costs of the other parties to the proceedings as well. This could be an amount in excess of one hundred thousand pounds depending on the number of parties involved. It is imperative that an applicant (or an objector) is advised of the potential risk of having a costs order against them. Readers are referred to Chapter 7 for what should be considered with a client from the outset, before an application is made in the Court of Protection.

10.3 – Reported cases on costs

The Court of Protection considered the factors set out in rule 19.5(2) of the Court of Protection Rules 2017 in the case of **Re JBN [2019]**.[145] In this case, the Public Guardian had made an application, without notice, seeking the revocation of a Lasting Power of Attorney on the grounds that the attorney had not acted in P's best interests. Following an investigation, the Public Guardian had concerns regarding a transaction involving the sale of P's property, the transfer of the majority of the sale proceeds (approximately £950,000) to the attorney and the attorney mixing his finances with those of P. According to the Public Guardian, this placed P at risk of not being able to fund his future care costs.

In the first instance, the District Judge suspended the Lasting Power of Attorney and appointed an interim deputy. The attorney contested the Public Guardian's application. His position was that at the time the property was sold and the sale proceeds were transferred to him, P had the capacity the make these decisions. The key issue in this case was whether

145 Re JBN [2019] EWCOP62.

P had the capacity to make decisions involving his property and affairs at that time.

The attorney was successful in getting the suspension of the Lasting Power of Attorney lifted. By the time the matter concluded, the attorney had incurred legal costs in the sum of around £82,000 and he sought an order that his costs are paid by the Public Guardian. In this case, the Judge departed from the general rule on costs after considering the manner in which the Public Guardian initiated the application and handled it. In particular, the Judge noted that the Public Guardian:

- had failed to give careful consideration to the evidence in respect of P's capacity before issuing proceedings. Had the Public Guardian done so, he would have concluded that the evidence was weak and insufficient to rebut the presumption of capacity;

- could have avoided incurring substantial costs by inviting the attorney to instruct a joint expert to determine P's capacity or asked the Court of Protection to decide on the issue of capacity in the first instance;

- sought orders of a very serious nature, such as the suspension of the Lasting Power of Attorney and the appointment of an interim deputy, without notice to the attorney;

- failed to recognise the attorney's cooperation to alleviate any concerns by offering to place funds in an account to cover all of P's care costs, thereby removing the risks of P not being able to fund his future care costs.

There has been an increase (although not a marked one) in the number of cases where the Court of Protection has considered or been asked to depart from the general rule on costs. From experience, the Court of Protection does not look favourably on a party who has wasted its time (as well as the other parties' time) by not following court directions at all or in a timely manner. In such circumstances, the Court of Protection is likely to make a costs order against that party.

The following factors would normally play a role in departing from the general rule on costs:

- Whether there were good reasons to start the proceedings.
- Whether proceedings were launched into disproportionately.
- Refusal to cooperate prior to the issue of proceedings.
- The reasonableness of a party pursuing an objection which has poor prospects of succeeding.
- The motive of a party: does it originate from personal grievance or out of a genuine concern for P?
- A party's disregard for any directions set by the Court of Protection which resulted to further and/or unnecessary costs being incurred.
- Unreasonable refusal to engage in alternative dispute resolution.
- Whether P's estate can afford the legal costs.

> Author's note – Given that costs are at the Court's discretion, one cannot always predict the outcome. It is therefore important for a party to carefully consider how they conduct themselves before and during the court proceedings. This can have a significant impact on the legal costs which a party may have to pay at the conclusion of a case.

10.4 – Recovery of costs

The Court of Protection will normally deal with the issue of costs at the conclusion of a case. A party who sought an order for their costs to be charged to P's estate should be advised that, if they are successful in securing such an order, their costs are likely to be assessed on a standard basis in the first instance. It is not unusual for a Judge to make the following costs order:

> *"The costs of the [parties] shall be subject to detailed assessment on the standard basis and the certified amounts of the same will be paid from the funds of [P]."*

The implication of such an order is that the party will not necessarily recover all their costs from P's estate. They will only recover the amount assessed by the Senior Courts Costs Office. It is therefore important to advise a client from the very start that even if the general rule provides for their costs to be charged to P's estate, they are not likely to recover 100% of their costs. They will be personally responsible for the shortfall – subject to any funding arrangement they have with their legal team.

There is a set procedure to follow when assessing costs on a standard basis which can take several months to conclude and involves incurring further costs. There are specialist costs experts specialising in the recovery costs in Court of Protection matters who can assist a party with the recovery of their costs. Once a Final Costs Certificate is issued, it is usually presented to P's attorney or deputy for property and affairs who will then reimburse the party for the costs they incurred in the court proceedings.

CHAPTER ELEVEN

CONSEQUENCES OF NOT SEEKING THE COURT OF PROTECTION'S APPROVAL

This topic is so vast that writing a separate Practical Guide on it would be justified. However, for the purposes of this chapter, the author will summarise the actions which can be taken against attorneys and deputies as well as the potential options available to redress the situation where P's assets have been gifted without seeking the appropriate approval.

11.1 – Ignorance is no excuse

Readers who are familiar with a Lasting Power of Attorney instrument will be aware that when it is made, attorneys are asked to sign the document and confirm their understanding of their duty to act based on the principles of the Mental Capacity Act Code of Practice.[146] Similarly, when applying for a Deputyship Order, deputies sign form COP4 giving undertakings which include having regard to the Mental Capacity Act 2005 Code of Practice and acting within the scope of the powers conferred on them.[147] However, in reality, when they eventually step up to their role, not many attorneys or deputies make time for reading and familiarising themselves with the Mental Capacity Act 2005 or its Code of Practice. As a result, very often, they end up taking actions which are unauthorised or unlawful.

146 See section 11 of a Lasting Power of Attorney instrument for further statements made by an attorney.

147 See section 4 of form COP4.

Attorneys and deputies are reminded that the Court of Protection will not sympathise with them simply because they were unaware of the scope of their powers. This was made particularly clear by Senior Judge Lush in the case of **Re Buckley [2013]**[148], when he commented *"Ignorance is no excuse."* Caselaw also shows that the Court of Protection is critical of such attorneys and deputies and will hold them accountable for their actions. In some cases, the Judge has even given permission to report the matter by naming the parties involved so that the public is made aware of what attorneys and deputies can and cannot do and what happens when they misbehave.[149]

11.2 – Being investigated by the Office of the Public Guardian

Where concerns about unauthorised gifting are raised with the Office of the Public Guardian which merit an investigation,[150] the attorney or the deputy will be subjected to an investigation. As part of their investigation, a Court of Protection visitor may arrange to meet with P to discuss the gift in question. The investigator may also interview the attorney or the deputy; seek disclosure of financial documents including bank statements and receipts; and review their management of P's property and affairs.

The investigator may conclude that the gift in question, although unauthorised, was made as a result of the attorney's or the deputy's genuine lack of awareness. If the situation can be redressed swiftly, the attorney or the deputy may be asked to return the gift to P. In addition, they will most likely be given a warning by the Office of the Public Guardian and their supervision may be increased to ensure that they do not breach their duty in the future.

---

148 Re Buckley: The Public Guardian v C [2013] EWHC 2965 (COP).

149 Re Joan Treadwell [2013] EWCH 2409 (COP) transcript, para 100.

150 The author addresses the issue of financial abuse and the investigations carried out by the Office of the Public Guardian in Chapter 12.5.

11.3 – Applying for the retrospective approval of a gift

If the gift is affordable and there appears to be some valid reasoning behind it, the Office of the Public Guardian may recommend that an application is made to the Court of Protection to ratify the unauthorised gift. Similarly, a practitioner advising an attorney or a deputy on an unauthorised gift which has already been made should suggest that an application is made to the Court of Protection for its retrospective approval.

This was one of the orders sought by P's deputy in the case of **Re MJL [2019]**.[151] In this case, the deputy had made modest gifts to several political organisations (the Labour Party, The Red Banner and Charter 88) which were not charitable organisations. Accordingly, the gifts fell outside the scope of the deputy's powers[152] and the Court of Protection's approval was required. The Judge dealing with the application considered several factors including the fact that prior to losing the capacity to manage his financial affairs, P had already put in place a standing order to gift to these three organisations and the gifts made were modest given the size of P's estate (which was in excess of £17m when the application was made). It was held that the gifts previously gifts made by the deputy were affordable. The Court ratified them and also gave the deputy the authority to continue gifting to the three organisations in line with the existing payments.

In contrast, the applicants in the case of **Re GM [2013]**[153] were not successful in obtaining the Court of Protection's approval of all the gifts previously made by them. In this case, at the conclusion of his investigation, the Public Guardian recommended to the deputies that they apply for

151 Re MJL [2019] EWCOP31. In this case, the application made by the deputy was not limited to the retrospective approval of modest gifts. The applicant sought several other orders including the making of substantial gifts from P's estate for the purposes of tax planning.

152 See Chapter 3.4 for a deputy's powers to gift.

153 Re GM [2013] EWHC 2966 (COP).

the retrospective approval of the money which they had given away on P's behalf. An application was made by the deputies and the Public Guardian was made a party to the proceedings. The Public Guardian was ordered to prepare a report on (a) how much had been gifted by the deputies, and to whom, and for what purpose; (b) exactly how much remained in P's estate, including the assets that would have passed to P on her daughter's death in 2010; (c) the Public Guardian's view on whether it would be appropriate for the Court to approve any of the gifts previously made by the deputies and, if so, to what extent; and (d) the Public Guardian's recommendations regarding the future of the deputyship.[154] The report prepared by the Public Guardian brought to light the fact that gifts previously made by the deputies came to a total sum of £231,259.50. In addition to this, the deputies had used P's monies to reimburse themselves a total sum of £46,552.24 for the purchase of extravagant items including the purchase of two motor vehicles and computers.

In this case, the Judge approved gifts totalling only £73,352 and the deputies became personally liable for the balance of £204,459.74. The Judge formed the view that the gifts were not in P's best interests for several reasons including the fact that the deputies had not consulted P prior to making these gifts and the gifts were completely out of character with any gifts P had made in the past.

This case shows that an application for the retrospective approval of a gift is not simply a box-ticking exercise. Each case turns on its facts and the advice remains that attorneys and deputies should seek the Court's approval *prior* to making an unauthorised gift. If they do not do so, there is no guarantee that the unauthorised gifts will be retrospectively approved.

154 Re GM [2013] EWHC 2966 (COP), para 20.

Author's note – Readers are reminded that the Public Guardian cannot approve a gift which falls outside the scope of an attorney's or a deputy's powers. Such approval can only be given by the Court of Protection.

11.4 – Being removed as the attorney or deputy

This section deals with the harsh penalties which attorneys and deputies may face for making unauthorised gifts. The Public Guardian or those concerned for P are known to take matters further and make an application to the Court of Protection to cancel or revoke a Power of Attorney[155] or a Deputyship Order, particularly in cases where large sums of monies have been misappropriated or gifted without the Court's approval.

Caselaw has shown that the Court takes a dim view of such attorneys and deputies and will not hesitate in replacing them. In the case of **Re EG [2015]**,[156] P had 4 children – one daughter and three sons. P had appointed her daughter and one of her sons as her attorneys for property and affairs. The daughter took an active role in the management of P's finances and gifted herself the sum of £15,000. She also gifted the sum of £20,000 to each of her three brothers, one of whom was her co-attorney. In total, the attorney had gifted the sum of £75,000 from P's modest estate resulting in P having only approximately £17,000 left in her estate. This was noted by the London Borough of Bromley who then raised concerns with the Office of the Public Guardian. The Office of the Public Guardian conducted an investigation into the attorneys' actions and subsequently made an application to revoke the Lasting Power of Attorney.

155 The Court of Protection can revoke a Lasting Power of Attorney under section 22(4) of the Mental capacity Act 2005.

156 Re EG [2015] EWCOP 6.

The attorney who had made the gifts to herself and her siblings objected to the Public Guardian's application. Her position was that P had capacity at the time the gifts were made. P was aware that her daughter was in financial difficulties and had agreed to help her out. According to the attorney, it was also P's wish for her other children to be treated equally, hence gifts of £20,000 were made to the other 3 children.[157]

The Judge did not accept this and found that the attorney had signed cheques in her capacity as an attorney; the gifts far exceeded the limited authority given to the attorneys; and they had breached their fiduciary duty by taking advantage of their position. The Judge also found that even though her co-attorney had not signed the cheques, he was still a party to the transactions. The Lasting Power of Attorney was revoked and the Court appointed an officer from the London Borough of Bromley as P's deputy to manage her property and affairs.

11.5 – Restoring P's estate by calling in the security bond

This is an option available where a deputy is appointed by the Court of Protection to manage P's property and affairs. When a deputy is appointed, in most cases, they will be ordered to obtain and maintain security. A Deputyship Order will usually not be issued by the Court of Protection until the deputy has purchased a security bond which is usually renewed every year for as long as the deputy manages P's financial affairs.

The purpose of the security bond is to insure the assets of P and it offers the guarantee to pay any financial losses suffered by P, up to a specific amount, as a result of the deputy's misconduct. The amount of security to be purchased by the deputy is normally set by the Court of Protection

157 In this case, the attorney had gifted herself the sum of £15,000 instead of £20,000 since she had previously received the sum of £5,000 from P.

at the time the Deputyship Order is made and depends on the value and the nature of P's estate.[158]

Where P's estate has suffered a loss as a result of a deputy making unauthorised gifts, in the first instance, the Office of the Public Guardian will seek to redress the matter swiftly by asking the deputy to return the gift to P.[159] However, in instances where the deputy cannot return the funds or the gift, an application may be made to the Court of Protection not only for the deputy's removal but also to enforce the security bond to cover the unauthorised gifts. If such an order is granted by the Court of Protection, the insurance company will restore P's estate up to the amount P is insured for and such payment will be made on demand and without further investigation. One can therefore appreciate why purchasing and maintaining a security bond is vital to ensure that P's estate is restored swiftly and without the need to embark on lengthy and costly litigation.

The calling in of a security bond was addressed in the case of **Re Joan Treadwell [2013]**.[160] This case is unusual since P had passed away before the application made by the deputy for the retrospective approval of gifts was heard by the Court of Protection. However, the Judge allowed the Public Guardian's application to call in the security bond, which was made a few months after P's death.[161]

In this case, P's son had been appointed as her deputy and he was ordered to obtain and maintain security in the sum of £200,000. A statutory will

158 The security bond is usually payable by P's estate, not from the deputy's personal funds.

159 See Chapter 11.2.

160 Re Joan Treadwell [2013] EWHC 2409 (COP).

161 The Court of Protection's jurisdiction ends upon P's death. Ordinarily, after P's death, P's personal representatives would apply to call in the security bond to restore the estate. However, since the Public Guardian was actively involved immediately before P's death, the Judge formed the view that the Public Guardian was best placed to make the application.

had been approved and executed in 2008 in which P left the residuary of her estate, which consisted mainly of capital which she had received from her husband, to her husband's two daughters from a previous relationship. The daughters were the deputy's stepsisters.

A year or so after the statutory will was made, P's deputy started making gifts to his side of the family. Over a period of three years, gifts in the sum of £59,375 were made by him. Although the majority of these gifts were made on customary occasions, the level of gifting and the total amount was unreasonable given that P's annual income was approximately £10,000 and some of P's capital was being used to make these gifts. It became apparent that the motive behind the gifts was to reduce P's available capital which in turn would reduce the amount P's stepdaughters would ultimately receive after her death, thereby frustrating P's testamentary wishes.

P died before the application for retrospective approval of gifts was heard by the Court of Protection and soon after, the Public Guardian made an application to enforce the security bond in respect of the unauthorised gifts. The application was heard by Senior Judge Lush. He considered all the relevant factors and found that the deputy could have made gifts of £1,000 a year to close family members and had he made an application seeking the Court's approval to make further gifts, the Court of Protection would have allowed him to make gifts up to £4,000 a year to family members. This was on the basis that P's needs were being met, her care was funded in full by the local NHS and she would have been left with an income of around £5,000 per annum to cover unforeseen expenses. The Judge therefore concluded that gifts totalling £15,000 over a period of 3 years could be ratified but the balance, being £44,375, were unauthorised gifts and P's estate should be restored accordingly. The Court ordered the enforcement of the security for that sum.

A more recent case on the calling in of a security bond is **The London Borough of Enfield and Matrix Deputies Limited and others** [2018].[162]

162 The London Borough of Enfield v Matrix Deputies Ltd & Anor [2018]

Matrix Deputies Ltd and its employees managed the property and affairs of several individuals. In 2017, the Public Guardian made a number of applications including seeking their discharge as deputies. Thereafter, a hearing was listed to consider applications to call in the bonds for certain individuals. This case is useful as it serves as a reminder the purpose of obtaining and maintaining a security bond[163] and sets out the steps involved in calling in a security bond which includes:

- The applicant providing a report, supported by documentary evidence, which identifies the loss caused by the deputy.
- The deputy will then have the opportunity to respond to the report.
- Thereafter, the Court of Protection will make a summary determination on the matter and confirm the amount of loss suffered by P.[164]
- If the loss suffered is less than the amount of the bond, the Court of Protection will clearly set out in the order the amount which the insurance company will be required to pay to P's estate. If the loss suffered is greater than the amount insured, the Court of Protection will order that the bond is called in for its full amount.

EWCOP 22 (24 September 2018).

163 The London Borough of Enfield v Matrix Deputies Ltd & Anor [2018] EWCOP 22, para 18 where the Judge refers to the comments made by HHJ Hodge QC that the purpose of the bond procedure is "to put in place a cheap, quick and simple mechanism to reimburse the incapacitatous party's estate in the event of a deputy's default."

164 The Court of Protection will not be expected to carry out a full forensic examination. This will be a matter for the insurer and the deputy should the insurer decide to pursue the deputy in the civil courts for the recovery of the funds they paid out.

Author's note – The main purpose of a security bond is to restore P's estate for any loss caused as a result of the deputy's wrongful act(s). Deputies should not assume that they will not be liable. They should be warned that the insurance company may decide to take legal action against them personally to recover the sums they paid out as well as their expenses. Furthermore, calling in a security bond normally applies to cases where a deputy is involved. This is not a remedy available in cases where an attorney caused a loss to P's estate since attorneys are not required to purchase a security bond.

11.6 – Pursuing a deputy or an attorney in the High Court

In situations where the security bond is not sufficient to restore P's estate or an attorney[165] has made unauthorised gifts and is either unable to return the gift or refuses to do so, proceedings can be brought against them in the High Court – either by P's litigation friend or the newly appointed deputy (during P's lifetime)[166] or by the personal representatives of P's estate (after P's death).

In the case of **Chandler v Lombardi [2022],**[167] P's daughter and attorney for property and affairs transferred P's property into the joint names of herself and P as tenants in equal shares. The attorney signed the relevant transfer document in her capacity as P's attorney and the form clearly

165 As a reminder, attorneys are not required to purchase a security bond and calling in a bond is not a remedy available when a loss is caused by an attorney's wrongful act.

166 This was one of the orders sought by the Public Guardian in the case of Re EG [2015]. The Court of Protection's authority was sought for the deputy to take such proceedings or steps as may be necessary to restore P's estate to the correct level.

167 Chandler v Lombardi [2022] EWHC 22.

stated that the transfer was not for money or anything that had a monetary value.

A few months later, when this came to light to P's son, he issued proceedings in the High Court, in his capacity as P's litigation friend,[168] to challenge the transfer of the property. In this case, the Judge found that it was neither necessary nor appropriate to make a finding as to whether P had the capacity to gift half of her property to her daughter since the daughter had acted and signed the transfer document in her capacity as P's attorney. The main issue, therefore, was whether the attorney had the authority to gift herself half of the property.

It was held that the gift in question was not an authorised gift pursuant to section 12 of the Mental capacity Act 2005 and the attorney should have made an application to the Court of Protection seeking their approval if she contemplated making such an extensive gift. The fact that she was not aware that she had to seek permission from the Court of Protection and was not informed by the solicitor who facilitated the transfer did not assist her case. It was found that the gift was substantial; it was made without consideration; and was a controversial and contentious step to take given the circumstances of the last two years of P's life. Accordingly, the Judge declared that the transfer of the property was void and ordered that the Proprietorship Register of the property be rectified.

> Author's note – In cases of financial abuse involving the revocation of a Power of Attorney or a Deputyship Order which results in the appointment of a new deputy, consider seeking an order authorising the newly appointed deputy to use P's funds to commence and conduct court proceedings in the High Court to restore P's estate.

168 P's son subsequently became the executor of P's estate after P passed away during the course of the High Court proceedings.

CHAPTER TWELVE

FINANCIAL ABUSE AND USEFUL CONTACTS

The author will conclude this book with a few useful tips and contact details on how to prevent and/or stop financial abuse. Recent reported caselaw and news articles making the headlines have brought to our attention the sad fact that financial abuse is on the rise. Such abuse can take several shapes and forms including unlawful gifting by an attorney or a deputy. This chapter addresses (i) how financial abuse is becoming a growing concern, (ii) how to detect financial abuse and (iii) who to contact to try and redress the situation.

12.1 – Financial abuse: a growing concern

There has been a distinct rise in the number of complaints made to the Office of the Public Guardian over the past few years and a large number of the rising complaints is in respect of an attorney's or a deputy's conduct regarding their mismanagement of P's financial affairs. As a reminder, the Office of the Public Guardian was established in 2007, primarily to safeguard the interests of P. The Public Guardian has a statutory power to supervise deputies[169] and part of their role is to carry out investigations where there are safeguarding issues and/or financial abuse concerns relating to deputies and registered attorneys.

To put matters into context, in 2018/2019, the Office of the Public Guardian carried out 2,883 investigations.[170] This increased to 3,099 in

169 Section 58 of the Mental capacity Act 2005.

170 OPG Annual report and accounts 2018 to 2019.

2019/2020.[171] There was a decline in the number of investigations carried out in 2020/2021 but this was mainly due to the Office of the Public Guardian not being able to accept cases for investigation during the pandemic when the risk of spreading the coronavirus disease was very high. With the easing of rules on social distancing post-pandemic, complaints and investigations are once again on the rise. The investigations carried out by the Office of the Public Guardian increased from 2,089 in 2020/2021 to 2,464 in 2021/2022.[172] The author anticipates that with family members and friends regaining physical contact with P in the post-pandemic period, the number of complaints and concerns will rise – not only in respect of an attorney's or a deputy's misconduct but also in respect of financial abuse inflicted by others.

12.2 – Spotting the signs of financial abuse

It is often thought that abuse takes place "*behind closed doors*" and is therefore difficult to identify. However, there are telltale signs which often indicate that someone may be taking advantage of P's vulnerability.

Those who are involved in P's care and the management of P's affairs – for instance P's family members; P's close friends; P's attorney or deputy; P's carers; the bank where P holds accounts; the local authority; care homes – are most likely to be the first ones to identify a potential misappropriation or mismanagement of P's affairs. The author lists below a few of these tell-tale signs and encourages readers to be vigilant and to watch out for them:[173]

---

171 OPG Annual report and accounts 2019 to 2020.

172 OPG Annual report and accounts 2021 to 2022.

173 This is not a non-exhaustive list and is derived from the author's experience and caselaw.

- Large or frequent withdrawals from P's bank account through the ATM.
- Adding someone else's name to P's bank account (without specifying they are P's attorney or deputy).
- Applying for credit in P's name.
- Non-payment of P's regular outgoings or utility bills resulting in lack of adequate food, heating or clothing.
- Non-payment of P's care home fees.
- Unexpected changes to P's Will.
- Controlling or restricting P's personal contact with others by turning visitors away.
- Controlling or restricting P's communications with others by denying P of their telephone and/or not allowing them to answer calls.

Matters of this nature can be emotionally charged and it is not uncommon for practitioners to receive enquiries from potential clients asking whether they can "take someone to court". Whilst court proceedings may be an option, it is important to explore other avenues in the first instance. In the next sections, the author lists other courses of action which should be considered before escalating matters to the Court of Protection or the High Court.

12.3 – Is there an attorney or a deputy?

Find out if P has a registered attorney or a deputy for property and affairs and inform them of your concerns. Since the attorney or deputy will have access to P's finances, they will be in a better position to look into the concerns raised and potentially stop financial abuse from taking place.

The Office of the Public Guardian keeps a register of Enduring Powers of Attorney which have been registered[174]; Lasting Powers of Attorney and Deputyship Orders. Anyone can apply to carry out a search of the register and this can be done by completing form OPG100. The applicant will be required to submit key information such as P's name, date of birth, address and the applicant's relationship to P. Following the application, the Office of the Public Guardian will confirm whether there is a registered attorney or a deputy to handle P's affairs or make decisions on P's welfare; when the Power of Attorney or Deputyship Order was made; and the name of the attorney or deputy.

A completed form OPG100 can be sent to the Office of the Public Guardian by email or by post and their contact details are:

Email: customerservices@publicguardian,gov.uk

Post: PO Box 16118, Birmingham, B2 2WH[175]

174 Unlike Lasting Powers of Attorney, there is no requirement for an Enduring Power of Attorney to be registered before it can be used. The Office of the Public Guardian will therefore not hold the details of an attorney appointed under an Enduring Power of Attorney unless the attorney registered it when the donor became mentally incapable.

175 Information stands correct as of November 2023.

12.4 – Interaction with the attorney or deputy

If your concerns relate to an attorney's or a deputy's own conduct, express these concerns to them directly. Very often, there is a simple explanation and suspicions can be easily cleared with open communication. However, it is important to be aware that attorneys and deputies owe a duty of confidentiality to P and are not likely to disclose personal or sensitive information relating to P, particularly if this would put P at risk of exploitation.

Although there is no obligation for them to respond to queries or concerns, registered attorneys and deputies are, however, accountable to the Public Guardian and the Court of Protection when ordered to do so.

12.5 – Contact the Office of the Public Guardian

If the attorney or the deputy appears to be unnecessarily secretive or defensive and refuses to clarify simple matters which are not likely to harm P or breach P's confidentiality, raise your concerns with the Office of the Public Guardian. As mentioned above, the role of Public Guardian includes investigating concerns and attorneys and deputies are accountable to him. The Office of the Public Guardian has a separate investigations unit and an investigator will usually look into matters; interview the attorney or the deputy as well as P in some circumstances and prepare a report.

It is important to note that the Office of the Public Guardian receives numerous referrals and will only investigate if there is a real concern regarding P. It is therefore advisable to put sufficient evidence before them to raise their suspicion. It is accepted that such evidence may not be easily available or will not be disclosed so as not to breach P's confidentiality. In such circumstances, it is advisable to "join forces" with other professionals (such as P's doctors, carers, close family members) who may have similar concerns. If the Office of the Public Guardian receives concerns from independent and unrelated sources, they are more likely to carry out an investigation, as evidenced in the case of **Re DP [2014]**.[176]

In this case, a social worker with the local NHS Foundation Trust first contacted the Office of the Public Guardian to express her concerns about the attorney's conduct after P had been found on a bus in a confused state.[177] The following year, a senior risk consultant with Aviva UK Life Financial Crime Team contacted the Office of the Public Guardian as he was concerned about the encashment of P's investment bond by the attorney. This led to an investigation being carried out by the Office of the Public Guardian which resulted in an application being made by the Public Guardian for the attorney to be removed and for a deputy to be appointed to manage P's financial affairs.

If the Public Guardian forms the view that there are valid concerns regarding an attorney's or a deputy's proposed conduct or the actions which they have taken, he may take several steps including:

- Imposing close monitoring of the attorney or the deputy and expect regular reports from them.
- Applying to the Court of Protection for an interim suspension of the Power of Attorney or the Deputyship Order whilst further investigations are carried out.
- Applying to the Court of Protection to revoke the Power of Attorney or the Deputyship Order.

---

176 Re DP (Revocation of Lasting Power of Attorney) [2014] EWHC B4.

177 Since the concerns related to P's health and welfare and the attorney was appointed to manage P's finances only, the Public Guardian felt unable to intervene. Instead, the NHS Trust placed P under a safeguarding alert.

- Applying for a deputy's security bond to be called in to restore P's estate if P has suffered a financial loss.

- Informing the police where a crime may have been committed.

To report a concern to the Office of the Public Guardian, email them at opg.safeguardingunit@publicguardian.gov.uk or telephone them on 0115 934 2777.[178]

The Office of the Public Guardian is unlikely to disclose their full report since it will undoubtedly contain information confidential and personal to P. However, they may provide limited information and a summary of their findings as well as inform the person who raised the concerns whether further action will be taken by the Public Guardian.

12.6 – Contact the Local Authority

Consider raising a safeguarding adult concern with the Local Authority responsible for the area where P is based, whether or not P is ordinarily a resident there.

Local Authorities have a duty to investigate matters where they suspect that an adult in their area is experiencing, or is at risk of, abuse or neglect.[179] This includes financial abuse which includes:

(a) *having money or other property stolen,*

(b) *being defrauded,*

(c) *being put under pressure in relation to money or other property, and*

178 Information stands correct as of November 2023.

179 Care Act 2014, section 42(b).

(d) *having money or other property misused.* [180]

The Local Authority will make whatever enquiries it deems necessary and will decide whether any action should be taken to protect P's position, such action to include referring the matter to the Office Public Guardian or to the police or making an application to the Court of Protection.

12.7 – Contact the police

The Fraud Act 2006 enables the police to take actions in serious cases of abuse and section 4 of the Fraud Act 2006 states that:

> "*(1) A person is in breach of this section if he –*
>
> *(a) Occupies a position in which he is expected to safeguard, or not to act against, the financial interests of another person,*
>
> *(b) Dishonestly abuses that position, and*
>
> *(c) Intends, by means of the abuse of that position –*
>
> *(i) To make a gain for himself or another, or*
>
> *(ii) To cause loss to another or to expose another to a risk of loss.*"

Attorneys and deputies hold a position of trust and if the concerns relate to their actions, consider referring the matter to the local police in addition to the other authorities mentioned above (such as the Office of the Public Guardian and/or the Local Authority). The police will get involved depending on the level of abuse which has taken place or is about to take place. As part of their investigation, they will interview the attorney or the deputy[181] (or anyone in a position of trust) and if there is

180 Care Act 2014, section 42(3).

181 In the case of Re Buckley [2013], Nationwide had referred the matter to the police and they interviewed and investigated the attorney in respect of

evidence that the person concerned has misappropriated P's funds, they may take further action including prosecuting the person who holds a position of trust.

12.8 – Making an application to the Court of Protection

Another option is to refer the matter to the Court of Protection and apply to remove the attorney or the deputy to stop further abuse from taking place. However, in the author's view, this should be the last resort given the legal costs involved and the limited evidence an applicant may have at the outset of a case.

As set out in Chapter 11.4, where financial abuse has been identified by the Office of the Public Guardian or the Local Authority, they are likely to take the lead in making an application to the Court of Protection. The person who initially raised the concerns may be made a party to the court proceedings and will therefore have the opportunity to set out their position during the course of the court proceedings.

Readers may find themselves in a situation where the investigations carried out by the relevant authorities (such as the Local Authority or the Office of the Public Guardian) are taking too long and there is an immediate risk of or ongoing financial abuse taking place. In such circumstances, it may be appropriate to make an application to the Court of Protection to initially suspend the relevant power of attorney instrument or the deputyship order. It is advisable for applicants to seek legal advice before making such an application.

---

the large withdrawals from P's bank account and the investment of those funds in a reptile business.

Author's final words...

Attorneys and deputies are reminded of their primary duty – to always act in P's best interests. Laws exist to protect vulnerable members of our society and caselaw shows that attorneys and deputies will receive harsh penalties if they misuse their power, whether done intentionally or not.

For those who are thinking of taking on the responsibility to manage someone's finances, the author strongly recommends that they familiarise themselves with at least the Mental Capacity 2005 and its associated Code of Practice and if in doubt, seek legal advice before agreeing to become an attorney or a deputy.

To those who have already been appointed as an attorney or a deputy, the author's message is to respect the laws and the codes and be mindful of the following 5 common pitfalls when making decisions on behalf of P:

1. Do not assume that P lacks capacity simply because they have been diagnosed with a medical condition.

2. A Power of Attorney instrument or a Deputyship Order does not give an attorney or a deputy unlimited power to make gifts or financial decisions[182] on behalf of P.

3. Even if a gift is authorised, attorneys and deputies should still make sure that they are affordable and go through the best-interests checklist set out in section 4 of the Mental Capacity Act 2005.

182 For instance, an attorney or a deputy cannot make a Will on behalf of P. They will require the Court of Protection's approval for this.

4. Not being familiar with the law is no excuse. An attorney or deputy who is not acting in P's best interests is likely to be penalised.

5. There is no guarantee that an attorney or a deputy who is a party to court proceedings involving P's property and affairs will recover their costs from P's estate.

MORE BOOKS BY LAW BRIEF PUBLISHING

A selection of our other titles available now:-

'A Practical Guide to the Independent School Standards – September 2023 Edition' by Sarah McKimm
'A Practical Guide to Estate Administration and Crypto Assets' by Richard Marshall
'A Practical Guide to Managing GDPR Data Subject Access Requests – Second Edition' by Patrick O'Kane
'A Practical Guide to Parental Alienation in Private and Public Law Children Cases' by Sam King QC & Frankie Shama
'Contested Heritage – Removing Art from Land and Historic Buildings' by Richard Harwood QC, Catherine Dobson, David Sawtell
'The Limits of Separate Legal Personality: When Those Running a Company Can Be Held Personally Liable for Losses Caused to Third Parties Outside of the Company' by Dr Mike Wilkinson
'A Practical Guide to Transgender Law' by Robin Moira White & Nicola Newbegin
'A Practical Guide to 'Stranded Spouses' in Family Law' by Mani Singh Basi
'A Practical Guide to Residential Freehold Conveyancing' by Lorraine Richardson
'A Practical Guide to Pensions on Divorce for Lawyers' by Bryan Scant
'A Practical Guide to Challenging Sham Marriage Allegations in Immigration Law' by Priya Solanki
'A Practical Guide to Digital Communications Evidence in Criminal Law' by Sam Willis
'A Practical Guide to Legal Rights in Scotland' by Sarah-Jane Macdonald
'A Practical Guide to New Build Conveyancing' by Paul Sams & Rebecca East
'A Practical Guide to Defending Barristers in Disciplinary Cases' by Marc Beaumont
'A Practical Guide to Inherited Wealth on Divorce' by Hayley Trim
'A Practical Guide to Practice Direction 12J and Domestic Abuse in Private Law Children Proceedings' by Rebecca Cross & Malvika Jaganmohan

'A Practical Guide to Confiscation and Restraint' by Narita Bahra QC, John Carl Townsend, David Winch
'A Practical Guide to the Law of Forests in Scotland' by Philip Buchan
'A Practical Guide to Health and Medical Cases in Immigration Law' by Rebecca Chapman & Miranda Butler
'A Practical Guide to Bad Character Evidence for Criminal Practitioners by Aparna Rao
'A Practical Guide to Extradition Law post-Brexit' by Myles Grandison et al
'A Practical Guide to Hoarding and Mental Health for Housing Lawyers' by Rachel Coyle
'A Practical Guide to Psychiatric Claims in Personal Injury – 2nd Edition' by Liam Ryan
'Stephens on Contractual Indemnities' by Richard Stephens
'A Practical Guide to the EU Succession Regulation' by Richard Frimston
'A Practical Guide to Solicitor and Client Costs – 2nd Edition' by Robin Dunne
'Constructive Dismissal – Practice Pointers and Principles' by Benjimin Burgher
'A Practical Guide to Religion and Belief Discrimination Claims in the Workplace' by Kashif Ali
'A Practical Guide to the Law of Medical Treatment Decisions' by Ben Troke
'Fundamental Dishonesty and QOCS in Personal Injury Proceedings: Law and Practice' by Jake Rowley
'A Practical Guide to the Law in Relation to School Exclusions' by Charlotte Hadfield & Alice de Coverley
'A Practical Guide to Divorce for the Silver Separators' by Karin Walker
'The Right to be Forgotten – The Law and Practical Issues' by Melissa Stock
'A Practical Guide to Planning Law and Rights of Way in National Parks, the Broads and AONBs' by James Maurici QC, James Neill et al
'A Practical Guide to Election Law' by Tom Tabori
'A Practical Guide to the Law in Relation to Surrogacy' by Andrew Powell
'A Practical Guide to Claims Arising from Fatal Accidents – 2nd Edition' by James Patience
'A Practical Guide to the Ownership of Employee Inventions – From Entitlement to Compensation' by James Tumbridge & Ashley Roughton
'A Practical Guide to Asbestos Claims' by Jonathan Owen & Gareth McAloon

'A Practical Guide to Stamp Duty Land Tax in England and Northern Ireland' by Suzanne O'Hara

'A Practical Guide to the Law of Farming Partnerships' by Philip Whitcomb

'Covid-19, Homeworking and the Law – The Essential Guide to Employment and GDPR Issues' by Forbes Solicitors

'Covid-19 and Criminal Law – The Essential Guide' by Ramya Nagesh

'Covid-19 and Family Law in England and Wales – The Essential Guide' by Safda Mahmood

'A Practical Guide to the Law of Unlawful Eviction and Harassment – 2nd Edition' by Stephanie Lovegrove

'Covid-19, Brexit and the Law of Commercial Leases – The Essential Guide' by Mark Shelton

'A Practical Guide to Costs in Personal Injury Claims – 2nd Edition' by Matthew Hoe

'A Practical Guide to the General Data Protection Regulation (GDPR) – 2nd Edition' by Keith Markham

'Ellis on Credit Hire – Sixth Edition' by Aidan Ellis & Tim Kevan

'A Practical Guide to Working with Litigants in Person and McKenzie Friends in Family Cases' by Stuart Barlow

'Protecting Unregistered Brands: A Practical Guide to the Law of Passing Off' by Lorna Brazell

'A Practical Guide to Secondary Liability and Joint Enterprise Post-Jogee' by Joanne Cecil & James Mehigan

'A Practical Guide to the Pre-Action RTA Claims Protocol for Personal Injury Lawyers' by Antonia Ford

'A Practical Guide to Neighbour Disputes and the Law' by Alexander Walsh

'A Practical Guide to Forfeiture of Leases' by Mark Shelton

'A Practical Guide to Coercive Control for Legal Practitioners and Victims' by Rachel Horman

'A Practical Guide to the Law of Driverless Cars – Second Edition' by Alex Glassbrook, Emma Northey & Scarlett Milligan

'A Practical Guide to TOLATA Claims' by Greg Williams

'A Practical Guide to Elderly Law – 2nd Edition' by Justin Patten

'A Practical Guide to Responding to Housing Disrepair and Unfitness Claims' by Iain Wightwick

'A Practical Guide to the Law of Bullying and Harassment in the Workplace' by Philip Hyland

'How to Be a Freelance Solicitor: A Practical Guide to the SRA-Regulated Freelance Solicitor Model' by Paul Bennett

'A Practical Guide to Prison Injury Claims' by Malcolm Johnson

'A Practical Guide to the Small Claims Track – 2nd Edition' by Dominic Bright

'A Practical Guide to Advising Clients at the Police Station' by Colin Stephen McKeown-Beaumont

'A Practical Guide to Antisocial Behaviour Injunctions' by Iain Wightwick

'Practical Mediation: A Guide for Mediators, Advocates, Advisers, Lawyers, and Students in Civil, Commercial, Business, Property, Workplace, and Employment Cases' by Jonathan Dingle with John Sephton

'The Mini-Pupillage Workbook' by David Boyle

'A Practical Guide to Crofting Law' by Brian Inkster

'A Practical Guide to the Law of Domain Names and Cybersquatting' by Andrew Clemson

'A Practical Guide to the Law of Gender Pay Gap Reporting' by Harini Iyengar

'NHS Whistleblowing and the Law' by Joseph England

'Employment Law and the Gig Economy' by Nigel Mackay & Annie Powell

'A Practical Guide to Noise Induced Hearing Loss (NIHL) Claims' by Andrew Mckie, Ian Skeate, Gareth McAloon

'An Introduction to Beauty Negligence Claims – A Practical Guide for the Personal Injury Practitioner' by Greg Almond

'Intercompany Agreements for Transfer Pricing Compliance' by Paul Sutton

'Zen and the Art of Mediation' by Martin Plowman

'A Practical Guide to the SRA Principles, Individual and Law Firm Codes of Conduct 2019 – What Every Law Firm Needs to Know' by Paul Bennett

'A Practical Guide to Adoption for Family Lawyers' by Graham Pegg

'A Practical Guide to Industrial Disease Claims' by Andrew Mckie & Ian Skeate

'A Practical Guide to Conducting a Sheriff Court Proof' by Andrew Stevenson

'A Practical Guide to Vicarious Liability' by Mariel Irvine

'A Practical Guide to Applications for Landlord's Consent and Variation of Leases' by Mark Shelton

'A Practical Guide to Relief from Sanctions Post-Mitchell and Denton' by Peter Causton

'A Practical Guide to Equity Release for Advisors' by Paul Sams
'A Practical Guide to Financial Services Claims' by Chris Hegarty
'The Law of Houses in Multiple Occupation: A Practical Guide to HMO Proceedings' by Julian Hunt
'Occupiers, Highways and Defective Premises Claims: A Practical Guide Post-Jackson – 2nd Edition' by Andrew Mckie
'A Practical Guide to Financial Ombudsman Service Claims' by Adam Temple & Robert Scrivenor
'A Practical Guide to Running Housing Disrepair and Cavity Wall Claims: 2nd Edition' by Andrew Mckie & Ian Skeate
'A Practical Guide to Holiday Sickness Claims – 2nd Edition' by Andrew Mckie & Ian Skeate
'Arguments and Tactics for Personal Injury and Clinical Negligence Claims' by Dorian Williams
'A Practical Guide to Drone Law' by Rufus Ballaster, Andrew Firman, Eleanor Clot
'A Practical Guide to Compliance for Personal Injury Firms Working With Claims Management Companies' by Paul Bennett
'RTA Allegations of Fraud in a Post-Jackson Era: The Handbook – 2nd Edition' by Andrew Mckie
'RTA Personal Injury Claims: A Practical Guide Post-Jackson' by Andrew Mckie
'On Experts: CPR35 for Lawyers and Experts' by David Boyle
'An Introduction to Personal Injury Law' by David Boyle

www.ingramcontent.com/pod-product-compliance
Lightning Source LLC
LaVergne TN
LVHW022054200926
848481LV00003B/906

* 9 7 8 1 9 1 4 6 0 8 6 4 3 *